1970s BRITAIN

Janet Shepherd & John Shepherd

SHIRE LIVING HISTORIES

How we worked • How

D1439652

SHIRE PUBLICATIONS
Bloomsbury Publishing Plc

PO Box 883, Oxford, OX1 9PL, UK
1385 Broadway, 5th Floor, New York, NY 10018, USA
Email: shire@bloomsbury.com

SHIRE is a trademark of Osprey Publishing, a division of
Bloomsbury Publishing Plc

© 2012 Shire Publications

First published in Great Britain in 2012 by Shire Publications

Transferred to digital print-on-demand in 2019
Printed and bound in Great Britain

A CIP catalogue record for this book is available from the
British Library.

Shire Living Histories no. 13. ISBN-13: 978 0 74781 097 1

Janet Shepherd and John Shepherd have asserted their
rights under the Copyright, Designs and Patents Act,
1988, to be identified as the authors of this book.

Designed by Myriam Bell Design, UK and typeset in
Perpetua and Gill Sans.

www.shirebooks.co.uk
To find out more about our authors and books visit our
website. Here you will find extracts, author interviews,
details of forthcoming events and the option to sign-up for
our newsletter.

COVER IMAGE: Shoppers in Regent Street on a hot
summer's day in June 1971. (Mary Evans Picture Library/
Gerald Wilson)

PHOTOGRAPH ACKNOWLEDGEMENTS
Mavis Battey, page 27; Pauline Bunyan, pages 10
(bottom), 25 (top); *Cambridge Evening News*, pages 6, 15
(top), 56 (top), 66, 67, 75; Cambridgeshire Collection,
pages 26, 56 (bottom); Colleen Cook, page 17; Cyprus
Tourist Board & Cyprus Airways, page 29 (bottom); Dry
Drayton Archive,

page 43; Getty Images, pages 4, 8, 12, 16 (top), 20, 37,
40, 52, 57, 59, 61, 62, 69; Imperial Tobacco Group, page
54; John Hinde Ltd, page 30; Kirklees Archive, pages 14,
23, 38; Gill McCorkindale, page 72 (bottom); Sandra
Lee, pages 45, 58, 68, 76; Sue Lusted, pages 18, 31;
Christine and Ken Parry, pages 16 (bottom), 22 (bottom),
50, 64; Pat Perry, page 46; Carolyn Powell, pages 34,
42 (bottom); Robert Opie Collections, pages 11, 24,
42 (top), 43 (top), 47, 48, 49 (top), 53, 70, 72 (top),
74; Gill Russell, pages 29 (top), 39; Emma Shepherd,
pages 30 (top), 44, 77; Janet Shepherd, pages 28 (top and
bottom), 32, 49 (bottom), 65; John Shepherd, pages 10
(top), 51; UK MOD Crown Copyright, page 22 (top);
Woburn Press, page 36.

AUTHORS' ACKNOWLEDGEMENTS
We are most grateful to the following for providing
photographs, information and assistance:

Mavis Battey; Caroline Blake; Elly Bradburn; Pauline and
Ernest Bunyan; Pat and Graham Carter; Sheila and Charles
Cole; Lesley and Ray Collier; Colleen Cook; Brenda
Corn; Mark Dunton; Sandra Lee; Jessica Livingstone;
Karen Livingstone; Susan Lusted; Gill McCorkindale;
Christine and Ken Parry; Pat Perry; Carolyn Powell;
Gill Russell; Emma Shepherd; Louise Shepherd; Flavia
Summers; Debra and Stephen Wade; Daniel Woodhouse;
and Maud and David Wyatt. Cambridgeshire Collection,
Central Library, Cambridge; *Cambridge News*; Cyprus
Tourist Board; Cyprus Airways; Dry Drayton Archive;
Getty Archives; John Hinde Ltd; Imperial Tobacco Group;
Robert Opie Collection; Robbins of Putney Ltd; Kirklees
Image Archive; UK MOD Crown Copyright; Woburn
Press (1973) *Till Death Us Do Part*, Johnny Speight.

Particular thanks to Gill McCorkindale for images, both
for this volume, and for *1920s Britain*.

A very special word of thanks to Les Waters, for
his expert technical assistance and advice and to our
commissioning editor, Ruth Sheppard, for her valuable
help and support.

Finally, thank you to the many family and friends,
especially in Dry Drayton, who assisted, or lent photos
which, for reasons of space, could not be included.

Shire ... woodland conservation charity, by funding the dedication of trees.

CONTENTS

PREFACE

IT WAS THE BEST OF TIMES, IT WAS THE WORST OF TIMES — Charles Dickens may have written this phrase about the years around the French Revolution, but it could — admittedly with a little exaggeration — also be applied to 1970s Britain. Though it saw the historic moment in which we voted by referendum to nail our colours to the European mast, it was certainly not Britain's finest hour politically or economically in other respects. No-one can forget that the decade ended with the election of Margaret Thatcher as the prime minister whose programme was unashamedly to sweep away what she saw as the abuses and wastefulness of the doomed post-war consensus.

Controversy dogged this decade — and it still does. Raging inflation, the three-day week and the 1979 winter of discontent often dominate discussion of these years, as do bell-bottomed jeans, mullet hair-dos and Pot Noodles. Yet recently — and perhaps to the surprise of many — the seventies have been voted the most stylish decade of the twentieth century, with its outrageous glitz of glam-rock, the equally outrageous fetish of punk-rock, and the quiet chic of Laura Ashley cotton prints and cheerfully modernist Habitat furniture.

There was always something interesting going on, and it affected not just the fashionable King's Road and the Television Centre, but changed the look of daily life and leisure time up and down the country.

Janet Shepherd and John Shepherd have brilliantly captured the kaleidoscope of these years that fall well within the memory of most middle-aged people today yet which seem — from the photographs and video archive — to come from the dim and distant past. As well as looking at life for all age groups across the social scale, at the fixtures and fittings of homes and high streets, they consider the deeper political and economic motors of change, when some of the tensions inherent in the post-war consensus were coming home to roost.

Peter Furtado
General Editor

Opposite: A nurse cares for a baby by candlelight during a 1970 power cut at St Andrew's Hospital, Dollis Hill, north London.

INTRODUCTION

THE CULTURAL, ECONOMIC, SOCIAL and political history of 1970s Britain is currently being subjected to detailed scrutiny by historians and social scientists. Traditionally, these years are often remembered as a time of recurrent crises, epitomised by poor economic performance, industrial unrest and political troubles. The British media, especially the tabloid press, reinforced perceptions of evident economic decline and industrial anarchy after a post-war 'golden age' of increased prosperity, rising living standards and relative industrial quietism. Among important contemporary studies of Britain published during the decade, Isaac Kramnick's volume especially captured the mood of 'Crisis Britain' in 1979, with its apocalyptic title *Is Britain Dying?*

Britain was often described as the 'sick man of Europe' – as 'ungovernable as Chile'. Seemingly all-powerful trade unions became the scapegoat for poor industrial relations, blamed by their opponents for contributing to the downfall of three British governments in 1970, 1974 and 1979. Union membership peaked at nearly thirteen million in 1979. Strikes, go-slows and industrial stoppages were labelled as Britain's 'national disease', seriously afflicting innocent and vulnerable people at home and at work. Militants, flying pickets, secondary picketing and work to rule became part of popular jargon. Memories of the industrial disputes, such as the bitter seven-week stoppage by postal workers, the miners' strikes and the Heath Government's State of Emergency – the 'three-day week', with rationed power cuts and candles – became entrenched in the national psyche.

Britain was also torn apart by episodes of political, social and racial strife. Thirteen civilians died on 'Bloody Sunday' in Northern Ireland in 1972, and the IRA bombing campaign was extended to the British mainland, including London's West End. Football hooliganism was seen as evidence of a decline in behaviour and educational standards among the nation's youth. Ethnic minorities suffered prejudice and

Opposite: On 18 October 1972, Professor Sir Alan Hodgkin (second from right), President of The Royal Society, opened the 5-km array as part of the Mullard Radio Telescope, then the most powerful instrument of its kind in the world. Radio Astronomy Observatory Lord's Bridge near Cambridge. In the background stands the One-mile Telescope, opened in 1964.

discrimination in housing, education, employment, and from racial attacks. There was also conflict with the police.

In 1973–74, the Organization of Petroleum Exporting Countries (OPEC) quadrupled crude-oil prices, resulting in a global crisis that shook western industrial economies. In Britain, a new term was coined – 'stagflation' – to describe the dual problems of increasing unemployment and soaring inflation that peaked at 27 per cent in the summer of 1975. In 1976, Britain had to apply to the International Monetary Fund (IMF) for a $3.9 billion standby loan after being engulfed in a sterling crisis, during which the pound depreciated significantly over several months.

As the decade drew to a close, 1.5 million public-sector workers – the greatest number since the 1926 General Strike – stopped work on 22 January 1979, a 'National Day of Action' in a public campaign for a national minimum wage. It was part of the wave of strikes and industrial stoppages that swept Britain during the last months of the Callaghan administration, the 'winter of discontent' from September 1978 to March 1979, which created iconic images of industrial

Bomb Squad officers search the wreckage of the tailors Gieves in Old Bond Street after an IRA bomb explosion, London, 27 January 1975.

anarchy during a harsh winter. Daily media coverage of strikes by Ford car workers, train drivers, road haulage workers, hospital staff, ambulance crews, civil servants, as well as mountains of uncollected rubbish, undug graves and unburied bodies, ignited great passions that resonated in British politics and society for decades.

Yet, a more balanced view would take into account Britain's position in a

Hits from 1970 and 1972. 'Bridge Over Troubled Water' by Simon & Garfunkel remained at the top of the charts for six weeks in 1970, becoming one of the decade's most memorable songs.

troubled world economy, beset by inflation and unemployment. In terms of international comparisons, British economic performance came largely midway between countries such as Australia, United States and Italy on the one hand, and West Germany, France and Japan on the other. In Britain, during most of the 1970s, more working days were lost through accidents and official illness than industrial stoppages. Big strikes (e.g. miners and car workers) were mainly concentrated in large plants in industrial areas. Other parts of Britain were relatively strike-free. In some years, over 90 per cent of industry had no significant stoppages. Trade-union support for government incomes policy (in reality wage restraint) was especially significant in reducing inflation between 1976 and 1978.

Moreover, there is also an alternative story to be told of 1970s Britain, not based largely on economic indicators. The think-tank, New Economics Foundation, published the *Measure of Domestic Progress* (*MDP*) in 2004, using different criteria, notably crime, family stability, pollution and inequalities in income. Remarkably, the *MDP* proclaimed 1976, the year of the IMF crisis, as the best time for Britons since 1950. This confirms the view that, for many people, life in 1970s Britain was relatively prosperous and enjoyable, witnessed in an exciting culture of popular music, colourful fashion styles, overseas travel and increased leisure opportunities.

In particular, these years can also be remembered for significant social and cultural changes in British life associated with sexual liberation, changing attitudes towards domestic violence, race relations and the beginnings of Green politics and environmentalism.

The decade saw the blossoming of the modern feminist movement that challenged norms in British society. In 1970, Kate Millet's *Sexual Politics* and Germaine Greer's seminal work, *The Female Eunuch*, appeared, and the first National Women's Liberation Conference took place in London. A year later, thousands joined a Women's Liberation

Royal Mail First Day Cover, commemorating Britain's entry into the European Economic Community, 3 January 1973. Despite hopes for economic advancement the immediate boost to British trade and employment was less promising in the 1970s due to global recession.

Souvenir programme from the Queen's Silver Jubilee celebrations held on 7 June 1977 in Thriplow village, Cambridgeshire.

march through London. There were also important pieces of social legislation: the 1970 Equal Pay Act (implemented in 1975); the Sex Discrimination Act, the Race Relations Act and, established to enforce these new laws, the Equal Opportunities Commission (1976). They were significant steps forward, although women still remained under-represented in British political life; the number of women MPs fell from twenty-six in 1970 to nineteen in 1979.

This was also an era of technological, scientific and medical progress that gradually transformed people's lives. For economic reasons, Britain cancelled its space programme in the early 1970s, but 1972 marked the opening of the largest radio telescope of its type in the world for the advance of radio astronomy. By the late 1970s, developments in computing and satellite communications foreshadowed the information technology revolution. Smoking was at last proved to be a serious health risk. Free contraception and legal abortions were both increasingly available. In 1978, an amazing medical advance was accomplished when the world's first 'test tube' baby was born in Britain.

The 1970s should not be written off as a cultural desert, nor as 'the decade taste forgot'. There were memorable 'modern classics' that have had a lasting impact on British culture in film, theatre, literature, music, art and television. In particular, British television was pre-eminent, probably the best in the world. American culture, in particular Hollywood, continued to have a significant impact on cultural life in Britain. 'Pop music' and the fashion world brought glitz and glitter to a decade often characterised by economic gloom, although much 1970s style has subsequently been judged as tasteless and vulgar.

On 1 January 1973, listeners to Radio 4's *Today* programme were greeted by 'La Marseillaise': Britain had joined the European Economic Community (EEC), with the hope of enjoying the economic advancement displayed by West Germany and France. Britain remained an important part of a global economy, although traditional imperial links with the British Commonwealth diminished as trade shifted to European partners.

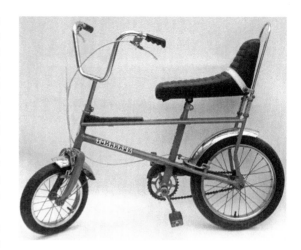

Raleigh Chopper Bicycle, the classic 1970s' 'must have' children's bike.

Global travel became more widely available. In 1976, the supersonic airliner Concorde began transatlantic flights to the United States. However, British roads became increasingly congested with more and more commercial and private vehicles, and the automobile industry suffered from stiff overseas competition, particularly from Japan.

The 1970s are also remembered for consumerism, fads and fashion. A random snapshot of British life might include the introduction of decimalisation in 1971, the 1974 arrival of McDonald's from the United States and by the end of the decade, the sight of chopper bikes and space hoppers everywhere. The summer of 1976 will always be remembered as the year of the famous drought. Sales of keg bitter and lager peaked, though wine was still less popular. Despite changes in lifestyles, social attitudes and beliefs, Britain retained many traditional values and institutions. In 1977, the Queen's Silver Jubilee was celebrated nationwide.

The story of *1970s Britain* is a nuanced history, rich in continuities and contrasts. It draws on a wide range of oral, documentary and media sources, illustrating the lives of those who lived, worked and played in Britain. The 1970s remain a memorable and significant era that has continued to influence and shape our lives and fortunes ever since.

WORK

B Y THE 1970s, the British economy was experiencing increasing difficulties and international pressures. The post-war boom (1940s–1973) – typified by a high demand for labour, full employment and the use of Keynesian management techniques by governments to even out economic downturns – had ended. Instead, following the 1973–74 OPEC international oil crisis, the trauma of stagflation was accompanied by increasing unemployment.

In August 1975, inflation peaked at 27 per cent, jeopardising the jobs and living standards of working people. By 1979, industrial growth had more than halved in six years. In terms of international comparisons, Britain's economic performance – on inflation, unemployment and productivity growth – generally fared badly compared to her main industrial competitors: France, West Germany, the United States and Japan. The decrease in Britain's share of world trade also continued, while import penetration increased. By the end of the decade, nearly 40 per cent of the UK's electrical goods was manufactured overseas.

The 1970s saw a striking shift away from manufacturing towards the service sector. Numbers working in manufacturing fell from around eight million in 1970 to below seven million in 1979, whereas employment in the service industries increased from twelve million to thirteen million.

There were marked changes in employment between different sectors of the economy. The numbers working in agriculture and industry declined; in agriculture from 3.1 per cent to 2.6 per cent, in industry from 43.8 per cent to 35.8 per cent. In contrast, those employed in the service sector, including banking, insurance and accountancy, grew from 53.1 per cent to 61.5 per cent.

Furthermore, unemployment rose from 676,000 to 1,289,000. Whereas 'full employment' – usually meaning less than 3 per cent of the workforce out of a job – was a general post-war norm, in 1971

Opposite:
'Fester' square,
1 February 1979.
A large rubbish
mountain in
Leicester Square
during the refuse
workers' strike,
'winter of
discontent',
1978–79.

and 1972 the number of workless exceeded 3 per cent and by 1974, 4.5 per cent. It continued rising year on year, finally reaching 6.2 per cent by 1979.

The UK car industry was a prime example of the difficulties being experienced by British manufacturing. In 1950, Britain was the world's greatest car exporter, second only to the USA in overall vehicle production. By the 1970s, the British car industry suffered from low profits, lack of investment and poor productivity. European

Construction on the M62 motorway, 1970. Initially, Britain's growing motorway network provided work in the construction industry, but from the mid-1970s, changes in transport planning and rising fuel costs curtailed much road building.

Cambridge Science Park. Biochemical firm L. K. B. Biochrom Ltd celebrate the dispatch of their first order, for a £13,000 biochemical research aid project, 22 March 1977.

cars, generally better designed and more reliable, became increasingly popular in the UK. In 1975, to save it from bankruptcy, the government nationalised the remaining UK major car producer, British Leyland, but the company's share of the domestic car market had still collapsed from 32 per cent to 20 per cent by 1979. By this time, imports accounted for more than half the car sales in Britain.

Similarly, the British steel industry, also affected by the general decline in manufacturing, experienced the most devastating years in its history. After the period of post-war expansion, and with a downturn in world production, British steel output declined from 28 million tonnes to 11 million tonnes per annum, causing the loss of around 100,000 jobs in a decade. By 1974, Britain had become a net importer, rather than exporter, of steel. There were similar stories in other strategic industries, such as shipbuilding, aircraft manufacture and engineering, which suffered from falling sales and job losses.

During these years, Britain also experienced unprecedented technological advances that altered people's jobs, working conditions and living standards. This became a major trend, particularly in Greater London and south-east England. Not for the first time, a 'north–south divide' was seen, based on job opportunities, health, housing and general standards of living, juxtaposing a generally prosperous south with a largely ill-fated industrial north.

The establishment of science and business parks

The Britannia Building Society was formed after a 1975 merger, becoming one of Britain's biggest mutual building societies with a large number of employees.

Britannia
Building Society
Ipswich Head Office

QUEENS HOUSE, QUEEN STREET
IPSWICH IP1 1SP

Member of the Building Societies Association
Telephone (0473) 86866
Authorised for Investments by Trustees

Slumberdown workers wrapped in their firm's quilts at Slumberdown's London Bond Street office during the 1974 power cuts.

in various parts of Britain was evidence of changing developments in the economy. These innovative enterprises provided fresh job opportunities based on new emerging technologies, the so-called 'sunrise' industries, combined with associated service sectors, such as banking and finance. By comparison, traditional staple, or 'sunset', industries, mainly in the north, were in decline as Britain's manufacturing base shrank.

Frigg Natural Gas Field, in the North Sea, in 1978.

The opening in 1970 of the Cambridge Science Park heralded a remarkable expansion of numerous small start-up companies, mainly associated with the University of Cambridge. 'The Cambridge Phenomenon', as it became universally known, was initially established with twenty-five firms in computer technology, but grew rapidly, bringing more than 40,000 workers into around a thousand or more new businesses in the Cambridge area, where previously there had only been a limited conventional electrical industry. A unique enterprise, parallel to California's famous Silicon Valley, this British development, comprising information technology, telecommunications, biosciences and associated services, provided self-sustaining and flexible job markets, and a high, albeit expensive, standard of living.

These employment trends were reflected in the patterns of trade-union development, with a significant expansion in the number of white-collar workers seeking to protect jobs and living standards in difficult times. By 1979, Britain's total union membership rose to nearly thirteen million. Key political developments also had important ramifications for the British economy and employment prospects. In 1973, Britain at last successfully became a member of the European Economic Community. Two years later, a national referendum confirmed the United Kingdom should remain a Community member.

From January to March 1974, Britain was subjected to an emergency 'three-day week' introduced by the Heath Government to conserve energy use in factories, offices and homes following unprecedented oil price increases and a pay dispute with the militant National Union of Mineworkers. Concentrating the working week into three days in this way arguably reduced British economic output by a fifth.

The Cambridge branch of SNOB, a popular 1970s chain of women's clothing shops, which employed local staff. A downstairs department, 'Rock Bottom', sold cheaper clothes. SNOB had its own shoe franchise called 'Revel'.

Braintree Fire
Station's open
day, late 1970s.
The first official
Fire Brigades
Union strike
was in 1978.
Two-thirds of
firefighters
worked a forty-
eight-hour week
of night and day
shifts, with their
low pay often
subsidised by
supplementary
benefits.

In 1975, the first North Sea oil was brought ashore, from the Argyll oilfield, by an American company, Hamilton Brothers. This historic development, resulting from the discovery of the giant Fortes oilfield in 1970 and the Brent oilfield, east of Shetland, in 1971, created new jobs in the construction and running of off-shore oil rigs, although the main benefits of this important natural resource from beneath the sea were not felt until the next decade.

The 1970s also witnessed significant changes in the size and structure of the British labour market, particularly the recruitment and employment of women. Between 1970 and 1980, the proportion of women in the workforce rose from 36 per cent to 40 per cent, compared to just 20 per cent in 1961.

Women's employment was affected by a number of key developments. The 1970 Equal Pay Act, a longstanding objective of the women's movement, was implemented in 1975 and was a direct outcome of the 1968 strike by women machinists at the Ford Motor Company's main Dagenham plant in Essex. Although only a small percentage of the Dagenham workforce, their pioneering action almost halted Ford car production across Britain. This new act gradually began to diminish gender differences in pay and employment conditions. The same year, the Employment Protection Act brought in maternity leave (up to 29 weeks with pay) and prohibited loss of employment owing to pregnancy. The 1975 Sex Discrimination Act covered employment, training and education to protect women and men against discrimination through sex or marriage. However, despite the work of the 1976 Equal Opportunities Commission, discrimination and gender inequalities remained major issues as it often proved difficult to bring cases to a tribunal.

Between 1971 and 1978, of approximately a million 'new for women' jobs, around 900,000 were part-time, with women comprising over 90 per cent of Britain's part-time workforce. Apart from teaching and nursing, the main opportunities for women's work were usually in manufacturing assembly work, or in the service industries, such as cleaning, clerical, catering, supermarket and shop work. In the vast majority of cases, this employment was part-time and lowly paid.

Although the number of women in work increased significantly, their position in British society only gradually improved. Typically, few women reached the higher echelons of business, law and medicine. At the BBC, a small number of women appeared on television as programme presenters, behind the cameras as producers or in senior management but, otherwise, they mainly occupied lower grades. A significant number of women undertook paid work at home, including clerical work, clothing manufacture and child-minding. In terms of unwaged work in the home, women remained predominantly responsible for housework and for the demanding role of providing primary care for children and elderly relatives.

The 'winter of discontent' was the epithet applied to the wave of strikes and stoppages between September 1978 and March 1979, beginning with the nine-week strike of the 57,000-strong Ford Company work force. Eventually, the dispute was settled with a 17 per cent pay rise. This shattered the government's rigid 5 per cent wages policy and acted as a pace-setter for other union demands during the annual round of pay claims. The following turbulent months of escalating pay claims and strikes seemed to embody popular perceptions, particularly portrayed by a hostile media, of a decade of unbridled union power and industrial anarchy. Many were reminded of the miners' strikes and energy crisis during early 1974. On 22 January 1979, the 'National Day of Action' by the four main public-sector unions saw 1.5 million workers demonstrate in London and other major cities against low pay and the government's stringent wages policy. However, within days, this uprising of low-paid workers in British society appeared to lose public sympathy when the Merseyside Gravediggers' Strike resulted in corpses being stored in warehouses. For many years, the events of the 'winter of discontent' have continued to resonate in the public memory and invoke an image of a troubled world of work and militant strikers in 1970s Britain.

TRAVEL AND TRANSPORT

THE 1970S WAS THE DECADE when international air travel became a reality for many Britons, rather than just the few. In particular, package summer holidays and winter breaks in the sun were made possible by cheaper flights to continental resorts. At home, car ownership increased for business, domestic and leisure purposes. However, overseas competition, particularly from Japanese car manufacturers, had serious consequences for the ailing British automobile and motorcycle industries. Despite some early 1970s growth in the motorway network, road congestion continued to increase, especially in many city and town centres.

Between 1970 and 1979, the number of air passengers doubled to around forty million a year. The buccaneering tycoon, Freddie Laker, dramatically cut the cost of air travel to beat his competitors. From 1976, Laker's Skytrain, flying from Gatwick to New York, offered flights at a third less than other airlines. 'My name's on every plane', boasted his adverts; satisfied young customers waved 'We Love You, Freddie' placards.

Regular transatlantic travel between Britain and the USA became commonplace. In 1976, the famous streamlined, supersonic passenger airliner, Concorde, a joint British–French venture, made its first flight between Europe and America. 'Fabulous, unique' Concorde broke the speed of sound, halving other airlines' times; its inaugural flight to New York in 1977 took just three-and-a-half hours. Although hundreds queued to view it at air shows, many bemoaned Concorde's enormous financial and environmental cost. In 1972, the Queen opened the Royal Air Force (RAF) Museum at Hendon, in north London, but the decade saw continued cutbacks to RAF commitments, notably in the Near, Middle and Far East.

The growth of international air travel led to demands for a third London airport to ease pressure on Heathrow and Gatwick. Various locations were considered, with Foulness in the marshy Thames

Opposite
The Anglo-French supersonic intercontinental airliner, Concorde, flew between Europe and the USA from 1976.

RAF Group Captain Peter McCorkindale OBE and Army Lieutenant Commander David Betley officiate at the 1975 handover of RAF Oakington, to the army, while a Victor tanker aircraft performs a flyover.

Estuary, chosen in 1971. Reactions were ambivalent. Local supporters welcomed high-speed rail-links to the capital and improved employment prospects, opponents cited increased pollution. However, plans were abandoned after the 1973–74 oil crisis and Stansted Airport was enlarged instead in the 1980s.

By the start of the 1970s, commercial sea traffic had decreased, but leisure cruises multiplied, bringing the heyday of the sumptuous ocean liner, *Queen Elizabeth 2*. Built on the Clyde, and operated by Cunard,

In July 1970, thousands watched SS *Great Britain* return to her home port of Bristol, after thirty-seven years on the Falklands seabed. Towed across the Atlantic, Brunel's ship arrived in Bristol Float Harbour on 19 July, exactly 127 years to the day after her 1843 launch.

the *QE2* was the last oil-fired passenger steamship to regularly cross the Atlantic.

By 1970, over half of British households possessed a car, from expensive Range Rovers to Reliant Bond Bugs. The Morris Minor remained a great learner car, easy to maintain and drive. However, home manufacturers, especially British Leyland, were increasingly affected by stiff foreign competition. By 1977, more than half the new car sales in Britain were of foreign vehicles. Volkswagen's Golf, the cheaper Czech Skoda, plus Ford's Granada and Fiesta were all popular. Global Ford, with manufacturing plants nationwide, was thought by many British people to be British, with its two-door sports car, the Capri, made in Liverpool, viewed as a top-selling 'British' vehicle. For some, a craze for 'Day-Glo paint and tartan interiors' in cars confirmed the 1970s as a 'tasteless' decade.

Motor caravans, especially Volkswagen camper-vans, were popular with a niche middle-class clientele for day and holiday use. At the top end of the market, the prestigious British firm, Rolls-Royce, was nationalised following bankruptcy in 1971 and its renowned car section was eventually sold.

In 1978, the renamed British International Motor Show was held outside London for the first time, at the new National Exhibition Centre near Birmingham. Intended to boost home sales, nearly a million visitors were able to view an array of new British models, with a Jaguar XJ-S as the centre-piece. However, the recent strike by their workers meant that Ford had no new models and was forced instead to display vintage cars.

By the 1970s, the British motorcycle industry faced overwhelming foreign competition, notably from Japan. Cheap Hondas virtually destroyed the British industry, leading to the demise of the West-Midlands

A typical small garage in the 1970s, Station Garage, Holmfirth, Yorkshire, 1977. Holmfirth was the setting for the TV series *Last of the Summer Wine*, 1973–2010. Bamforth saucy seaside postcards were also produced here.

"Don't cross near parked cars"
says Kevin Keegan

BE SMART
BE SAFE

Use the Green Cross code

RKD 81 ON

Poster for the Green Cross Code road safety campaign (1976), featuring football star Kevin Keegan, one of a number of celebrities who supported the campaign.

motorcycle manufacturer, Norton Villiers Triumph, in 1978.

As road traffic increased, city centres became more hazardous, with enormous European lorries becoming a common sight. Motorcycle accidents increased dramatically. Due to the increase in pedestrian accidents, the Royal Society for the Prevention of Accidents launched a new children's road safety campaign, the Green Cross Code (1970), promoted by famous sports personalities.

The 1973 energy crisis resulted in the imposition of a universal speed limit of 50 miles per hour; later this became 30 mph in built-up areas, 60 mph on single carriageways and 70 mph on dual carriageways and motorways. Breathalysing drivers suspected of excess drinking had already improved accident statistics. Despite government advertising during the 1970s, seat belts were not compulsory until 1983; controversially, popular television 'cops' from ITV's *The Sweeney* did not wear them.

There were a thousand miles of British motorways by 1972, the longest being the M6. The best-known motorway landmark was the complex interchange near Birmingham, completed in 1972 and nicknamed 'Spaghetti Junction'. After the 1973 fuel crisis, motorway construction slowed, with some schemes abandoned. The M5 was only completed in 1977, fifteen years after the start of construction. Mounting costs and fierce opposition stopped plans for London ringways and the widening of the capital's congested Archway Road. However, from 1979, the new Thatcher government supported more road projects, marking the start of numerous upgrades. Quiet country roads could still be found but many old towns, with narrow streets, became increasingly clogged as the volume of road traffic grew.

Many car-less households still relied on public transport: buses, trains, and – in London and Glasgow – underground systems. In fifty metropolitan districts local government monopolies ran essential bus services. Some major towns provided large subsidies to keep fares low and built modern bus stations, as in Huddersfield in 1972. In Bradford, the last trolley-bus system in Britain closed the same year.

A quiet country road, Thriplow, Cambridgeshire. A Morris Minor estate car meets a herd of cows, c. 1970s.

The increase in car ownership led to a decline in bus services, particularly affecting isolated rural communities. In the capital, many bus services had passed from London to National Bus Company control in 1970. By 1971, new one-man-operated buses brought staff reductions but in 1974, London appointed its first female bus driver since the Second World War. In attempts to win passengers back to travelling by bus, London Transport launched new Silver Jubilee buses in 1977 and a year later, Birmingham displayed its ultra-modern Metrobus at the Motor Show. By 1979, the incoming Conservative administration controversially began a programme of bus deregulation and privatisation.

Meanwhile, Britain's rail network also continued to decline. British Rail (BR) had run the nationalised rail system since 1948 but Britain lagged behind Europe for dieselisation and electrification. The massive 1960s line closure programme, the 'Beeching Axe', initiated by BR chairman Dr Beeching, continued; by 1975, when the National Railway Museum opened in York, only 2,000 stations and 12,000 miles of usable track were left. Yet the system remained unprofitable.

The decade did see some new rail investment. From 1970, electric trains ran between Glasgow and London and high-speed diesel services (HST) attracted more passengers. The famous Intercity 125 HST came into service in 1976 on Great Western and East Coast main lines; speeds up to 100 mph cut an hour off the journey from London to Edinburgh. Initially an interim measure, the 125 HST remained after plans to introduce the tilting Advanced Passenger Train were cancelled. Memorable BR posters

Postcard from the 1970s showing the Civic Centre, Plymouth, Devon, with the town's distinctive red double-decker buses.

promoted 'away days', and 'supersavers'. Passengers were urged to take the Intercity 125 'to York Races and save £1' or travel by rail to the theatre – 'That's enter*train*ment!'

The two British underground systems, in Glasgow and London, had nineteenth-century origins. By the 1970s, the Glasgow Subway was badly run down. Major refurbishment was undertaken between 1977 and 1980, with students at the Glasgow School of Art responsible for the design of the modern bright orange carriages.

From 1970, London Transport ran the capital's underground system and introduced much-needed new development, such as the Victoria line. Pimlico Station opened in 1972 and by 1974 the Victoria line had reached Brixton. With the growth of foreign travel, the Piccadilly line was extended to Heathrow Airport in 1977. By 1979, the 'state of the art' Jubilee line had opened; initially called the Fleet line, it followed London's hidden Fleet River. Automated 'mind the gap' public announcements, notably at Bank and Piccadilly stations, were heard from 1970, famously warning about the space between the train and the platform.

On 28 February 1975, the Moorgate Tube Disaster caused the greatest loss of life on the London Underground since the Second World War. A Northern line train overran the station platform and crashed into the end of the tunnel. Forty-three people, including the driver, were killed instantly; others died in hospital. The London Fire Brigade and hospital medical staff worked valiantly at the scene recovering the bodies of victims over several days. Afterwards, to prevent similar tragedies, an automatic stopping system, the 'Moorgate Control', was introduced on all underground trains. The Moorgate accident was one of the most tragic episodes in British public transport history.

Cambridge Railway Station, c. 1970s. The long classical façade is Grade II listed.

FAMILY LIFE

IN GENERAL, THE 1970S WITNESSED an overall improvement in most people's living standards and significant changes to British family life. Families with a male breadwinner largely remained the norm, but increasingly, hardworking mothers also took on part-time work outside the home. In particular, a marked rise in the use of contraception by women reduced family size compared to previous generations. The number of single-parent families also gradually grew. There was also a rise in the divorce rate, reflecting changing attitudes and lifestyles in a more permissive society. Unemployment, poor housing and debt often contributed to marriage breakdown. With cheaper flights, more families headed for Spanish beaches than domestic promenades as foreign breaks in the sun supplanted traditional British seaside holidays.

Declining birth rates kept Britain's population virtually static. Women were having babies later than their mothers. Contraception, especially the contraceptive pill, was freely available from the early 1970s to single, as well as married, women and the '2.4 children' family became commonplace. By 1974, the overall number of women using 'the pill' had reached four million. Yet a 1978 Family Planning Association report noted that, despite free family planning advice, contraceptive advertisements were still prudishly banned on London Transport and commercial television. Perhaps surprisingly given the increased use of contraception, the number of illegitimate children rose, although from 1975, their inheritance rights were protected.

The Watson family celebrate Christmas, Sheffield, 1973. The family were variously employed in the Post Office, a local printers, in teaching and at home. One son was completing a degree at Sheffield Polytechnic; the youngest was at school.

The Livingstone family, outside their home in Marriott Road, High Barnet, Hertfordshire, 1978.

Space hoppers became popular among children across Britain during the 1970s.

Children's needs received more attention. The Child Poverty Action Group highlighted the plight of a growing number of poor children. Local communities like Stoke Newington in north London established childcare facilities: nurseries, toy libraries, and adventure playgrounds. Pre-school provision, comprising playgroups and mother-and-toddler groups, improved. One goal of the women's movement was twenty-four-hour playgroups and feminist Catherine Hall opened a Women's Liberation Playgroup in Birmingham.

Growing awareness of physical dangers led to more child-safety equipment becoming available – baby alarms, car seats and bicycle helmets – as non-supervised outdoor activities for children declined. The popular Mothercare chain of shops thrived as demand soared for improved baby products; and better 'disposables' gradually began to replace towelling nappies. 'Home makers' were still predominantly women. Women's Liberation posters of the time demanded 'Wages for Housework' and, beneath an image of an ironing board, '*Strike* While the Iron Is Hot!'

Parental priorities increasingly focused on good health and academic achievement, with greater analysis of how their children (popular names included Sharon, Tracy, Wayne, Steven) should be raised. Every seven years, Granada TV's *Up* series tracked the effect of class on fourteen children who were seven at the time of the first programme in 1963; the two 1970s follow-ups, *7 plus Seven* (1970) and *21 Up* (1977), were hugely popular but criticised for a lack of impartiality. By mid-decade, the liberal 1960s legacy in parenting had waned and in *Raising Children in a Difficult Time* (1974), famous paediatrician Dr Spock urged a return to firmer discipline. However, mothers interviewed for *The Changing Face of Motherhood* 2011 research project, many of whom were themselves parented in the 1970s, regarded the decade as 'less pressured', as fewer than a quarter of mothers worked outside the home in 1971.

An increasing emphasis on child welfare exposed a darker side to childhood. The tragic life and death of seven-year-old Maria Colwell horrified the nation and Maria's name has remained in the public

The village wedding of Margaret Wyatt and John Swift, Dry Drayton, 13 August 1977. All the bridesmaids wore Laura Ashley dresses.

consciousness ever since. Despite concerns raised by neighbours and teachers, Maria was abused in her Brighton family home until she was eventually killed by her stepfather in 1973. The tragedy was widely reported, leading to a public inquiry.

Attitudes to marriage and divorce were changing. 'Marriage for life' was increasingly challenged as more couples separated. From 1 January 1971, the Divorce Reform Act permitted divorce on the sole grounds of 'irretrievable breakdown', without necessity to prove 'fault'. Couples could divorce after a two-year separation; divorce applications soared, exceeding a hundred thousand for the first time in the year 1971–72.

In 1971, the world's first women's refuge for battered women was opened in Chiswick by pioneer activist, Erin Pizzey; by 1974, the National Women's Aid Federation was established. The subject of violence in marriage led to the first Domestic Violence and Matrimonial Proceedings Act (1976), which enabled victims to obtain court orders against violent partners. A year later, the first Rape Crisis centre opened in London.

Cyprus Airways and the Cyprus Tourist Board combined to entice holidaymakers to the Mediterranean island with this c. 1970s poster.

The island no-one ever forgets.

Cyprus Airways

CYPRUS
no-one comes once

29

Members of the extended Shepherd family gather on Ramsgate beach during their annual day-trip to the seaside, c. 1979.

Debt increasingly became an issue for many families. By the mid-1970s, inflation had reduced savings and the lower value of the pound meant many middle-income families had to limit their spending. Credit cards provided a quick route to 'ready money', as banks encouraged a 'buy now pay later' culture. In 1972, Access credit card, 'your flexible friend', arrived, rivalling the established Barclaycard. Unsolicited plastic cards arrived in the post, ready for signature and immediate use. Despite many objections, this 'inertia method' led to a growth in credit-card use. 'Taking the waiting out of wanting' joined the nation's vocabulary. By 1973, credit-card holders found they were compelled to repay 15 per cent of their balance each month; a crippling burden for some. Nationwide, Citizens' Advice Bureaus were overwhelmed with enquiries about unemployment and debt.

Despite inflation, the number of people taking foreign holidays, with guaranteed sunshine, increased. In 1971, the *Daily Mail* advertised 'winter breaks in Spain for £14, including all meals' and 'long weekends in European cities for £19'. From 1970, insurance was available against travel firms collapsing, such as Clarksons and Horizon in 1974, the year ITV launched its informative *Wish You Were Here...?* holiday programme. By 1979, with inflation dropping and disposable incomes rising, the number of Britons holidaying abroad reached a new record.

This c. 1970s postcard depicting Butlin's Holiday Camp, Filey, North Yorkshire seems to clearly show the declining numbers choosing this type of holiday.

BUTLIN'S FILEY—*A General View*

Photo: E. Ludwig, John Hinde Studios.

Some middle-class families even began taking two annual holidays, one abroad, one at home. For others, like the Livingstones, with two adults and three daughters on one teacher's salary, foreign holidays were out and a camping holiday at Cerne Abbas was saved for all year.

Days out became more exotic, as new safari parks attracted millions of visitors; by the mid-1970s, seven had opened. Some families still enjoyed trips to the coast and in 1979, daring Brighton established Britain's first nudist beach. However, despite the introduction of two new bank holidays (New Year's Day from

Three-year-old Catherine Lusted meeting the donkeys at a wildlife centre on the Isle of Wight, c. 1975.

1976; May Day from 1978), British seaside holidays declined. Holiday camps still attracted those on limited budgets but their heyday was over. Memories of Butlin's at Minehead in the 1970s included the inconvenience of 'little chalets, with loos and baths in a separate block. Radio Butlins woke you up in the morning'. Fire badly damaged the end of the 'longest pier in the world' at Southend in 1976. Static caravan parks still drew visitors but the caravan industry – along with hotels and 'bed and breakfast' establishments – was adversely affected by the 'foreign package holiday'. Tourism in Northern Ireland suffered both from the overseas holiday boom and the fear of IRA bombs.

Religious observance continued to fall, despite senior clergy alleging that attendance at Sunday services eclipsed declining Saturday football crowds. The number of baptisms and confirmations dropped; by 1976 a redundant church was demolished 'every nine days'. Huddersfield's new Baptist Church in 1973, featuring an organ with a state-of-the-art digital computer, was an exception. With society more affluent and more secular, 'here and now' often took precedence over 'hereafter'. In the 1978 Reith Lectures, Dr Edward Norman fruitlessly urged the nation to 'abandon worldliness' and 'contemplate the soul'. In Northern Ireland, bitter sectarian divisions and violent conflict alienated even more families from the church.

Outside mainstream religion, the 1977 Olympia Festival of Mind and Body celebrated a 'New Age', with numerous stands promoting yoga, transcendental meditation, astrology, metaphysics and even witchcraft.

HOME AND NEIGHBOURHOOD

ONE OF THE PREDOMINANT FEATURES of 1970s Britain was the dramatic change in both public and private housing sectors in different parts of the country. Soaring house prices, particularly in London and the south, made it difficult for many young couples to get onto the property ladder. Meanwhile, wealthier middle classes and professionals could afford new suburban homes, with the latest equipment. During these years, rents rose significantly for those on council estates, including the dismal high-rise blocks that still often characterised local authority accommodation.

Inflated house prices made it hard to obtain affordable mortgages, or even save for the necessary deposit. In 1970, the average cost of a

A typical sought-after 1970s four-bedroom detached house, with porch and garage, photographed in 2011.

A child's jigsaw showing a typical 1970s living room, with paved hearth surround, 'bucket'-style chair, formica table, small TV in wooden casing, pouffe and fitted carpet.

'three-bed semi' was around £5,000 but prices quickly rose. The Livingstone family struggled to buy a four-bedroom 'thirties' house in north London in 1970; with a tight budget, the 'newly installed central heating was rarely on'. Prices rocketed again and the Livingstones sold the same house for £19,000 in 1977 but had to pay £27,000 for their next, only slightly larger, property.

Double-salaried young professional couples seeking ideal homes frequently preferred new properties, with patios, large insulated picture windows and garages. Many living–dining areas were divided by arches, glass doors or open-plan storage units. Carpets were fitted; autumn-coloured 'shag pile' was seen everywhere. The 1970 Ideal Home Exhibition featured stone-surround fireplaces and the modern fuel: smokeless Coalite. Most homes had a washing machine; soon many were 'built-in' but, like freezers, were expensive: a 1977 Electra (the national Electricity Board's own brand) fridge freezer cost £200. By 1971, 91 per cent of homes had a television but the new 'must have' was colour. Currys advertised 'music centres', comprising 'automatic turntables, audio cassettes and stereo VHF radios'. By 1979, most people had landline telephones. The first video recorders, digital watches, pocket calculators and Sony Walkmans arrived late in the decade. Early home computers were in only a minority of homes after 1978.

Ultra-modern design became crucial; Victorian fireplaces were ripped out, antique chairs painted white. Artex, a sought-after stippled coating for walls and ceilings, later fell out of fashion, as did 'avocado bathrooms' – in 2008 voted 'the most tasteless design feature of all time'. For many, Mike Leigh's classic suburban satire, *Abigail's Party* (a BBC TV's Play For Today in 1977), essentially captured the aspirant 1970s. This 'cocktail party from hell' starred Alison Steadman as the pretentious hostess, Beverley, offering bad taste alongside cheese and pineapple chunks.

Elsewhere, in the children's Ladybird book, *The Hotel*, a room-maid straightens a bed with sheets, blankets and a 'padded eiderdown', forerunner of the continental quilt. Novelty lava lamps still sold well and painted plaster flying ducks decorated many walls – remembered as Hilda Ogden's choice in ITV's *Coronation Street*. The show's northern-street culture attracted an ever-growing audience, reaching its thousandth episode by 1970.

For the less well-off, housing options were limited. War damage was still evident in Liverpool city centre and some other cities. Victorian terraced properties in Manchester's Moss Side were only gradually being replaced by newer, and then often unaffordable, housing. Glasgow's slum clearance continued into the 1970s; large parts of the notorious Gorbals district were demolished, while groups like 'Facelift Glasgow' restored older properties. In 1973, two million properties were still without 'an inside toilet, bath or running water', as was Father Christmas in Raymond Briggs' hugely popular 1978 children's book. In Papworth, Cambridgeshire, some elderly people refused flush toilets when mains sewage arrived in the 1970s.

By the end of the decade, a third of all Britain's housing was council-owned. New building standards ensured recent properties were more generously proportioned, but many families still lived in cramped accommodation on sprawling 1950s estates. Fewer high-rise blocks were built after the partial collapse of Newnham's Ronan Point in 1968, caused by structural defects. Leeds' Quarry Hill estate, featured in the

A pupil's description of his middle-class home in Mowbray Road, Cambridge. c. 1979 .

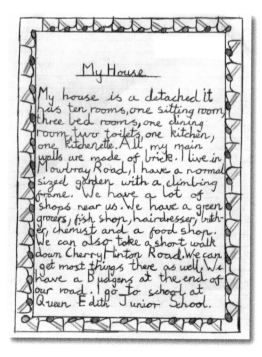

My House

My house is a detached it has ten rooms, one sitting room, three bed rooms, one dining room two toilets, one kitchen, one kitchenette. All my main walls are made of brick. I live in Mowbray Road, I have a normal sized garden with a climbing frame. We have a lot of shops near us. We have a green grocers, fish shop, hairdresser, butcher, chemist and a food shop. We can also take a short walk down CherryHinton Road. We can get most things there as well. We have a Budgens at the end of our road. I go to school at Queen Edith Junior School.

1970s ITV sitcom *Queenie's Castle* (starring renowned British actress Diana Dors), also had construction problems and was demolished in 1978. London's Elephant and Castle Heygate estate (1974) was notoriously described as a 'Warsaw suburb'. Social problems associated with high-rise living were becoming apparent. Tenants on Sheffield's Hyde Park reported 'isolation' and depression. Play facilities for children were often poor, and improving, or changing, accommodation was difficult. Tottenham's poorly designed Broadwater Farm, completed in 1971, was not adjacent to any underground stations; by 1979, its all-white tenants' association was unrepresentative of an estate where nearly half the population was from ethnic minorities.

The 1972 Housing Finance Act introduced higher, 'market', rents for council homes, adversely affecting poorer families. Derbyshire's Clay Cross councillors (later personally bankrupted) refused to implement rent rises, abandon free school milk or cancel television licences for the elderly. Clay Cross streetlights remained on throughout the miners' strike, defying the government's plea to 'Switch Off Something'. In an episode of BBC 1's *Till Death Us Do Part*, in London's Docklands, right-wing Alf Garnett's socialist daughter Rita switched on all the electrical appliances, crying, 'We're helping the miners!'

Labour's 1977 Housing Act was an important advance, creating national local authority guidelines for the homeless. However, there were fewer council properties for rent after 1979 when Margaret

This 1976 jigsaw box shows a 1970s street scene, with corner shop. Carl Giles was famous for the *Daily Express* Giles family cartoons. His infamous character, Grandma', is in the shop doorway.

Thatcher's new flagship policy gave tenants the 'right to buy' their own homes.

The 1972 Local Government Act established two-tier county and district councils, leading to many new county and metropolitan boroughs. Some towns 'moved' – after over a hundred years as a borough council, Huddersfield, with its striking new architectural Queensgate market, was incorporated into Kirklees Metropolitan District. After centuries in Hampshire, Bournemouth became part of Dorset. New town Milton Keynes, with its modern grid system and vast European-style shopping centre, continued to grow.

Growing immigration, swelled in 1972 by expelled Ugandan Asians, led to increased racism, both institutional and on the street. Conservative MP Enoch Powell called unsuccessfully for voluntary repatriation. The far right anti-immigrant National Front (NF) gained over ten per cent of the vote in some 1974 London council elections. By 1978, when the first anti-racist 'Rock Against Racism' concert was staged, there were nearly two million Commonwealth immigrants. The 1977 Commission For Racial Equality gave anti-racism a higher profile and the death of anti-fascist Blair Peach, possibly struck by the police at a 1979 anti-NF demonstration, reverberated for decades. In 2011, apologies were still being sought from the Home Office for compulsory 'virginity tests' endured by Asian immigrant women in the late 1970s.

The cover of a book of Johnny Speight's scripts for BBC I's *Till Death Us Do Part* sitcom, 1973. Alf Garnett (seen speaking) frequently expressed outrageous prejudiced and racist opinions.

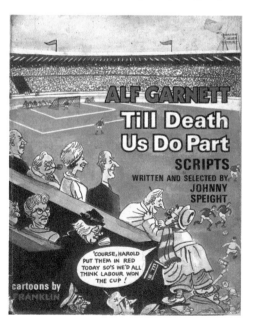

Policing in general was increasingly challenging and open to criticism, especially after a minority of prejudiced police regularly used 'sus' (stopping suspects), without sufficient cause. A 1972 survey of West Indians, in London and Nottingham, found 'a third thought the police discriminatory'. Public relations improved when the capital's police force, the Metropolitan Police (the 'Met'), enrolled women for the first time, and they were praised for their careful handling of the 1975 IRA Balcombe Street Siege and 'Spaghetti Siege' robbery. However, many of the general public thought 'crooks were getting away with it' and demanded harsher sentencing. ITV's *The Sweeney*, in which police regularly bent rules to

The 'new town' of Milton Keynes famously acquired a herd of concrete cows in the late 1970s, created by an artist-in-residence.

'catch their man', had high approval ratings. Tourists in London, considered a 'safe city' in 1970, were by 1979 comparing it unfavourably with New York, as muggings and burglaries increased.

In 1975, cricket fans arriving at Headingley, Leeds, for the third Ashes Test final against Australia, found the pitch vandalised and slogans reading 'George Davis Is Innocent, OK?' – part of a successful direct-action campaign to free wrongfully convicted mini-cab driver, George Davis, later correctly imprisoned for other bank robberies. Far more frightening was the case of Peter Sutcliffe, the 'Yorkshire Ripper', who terrorised northern England, murdering eleven women between 1975 and 1979 and another two in 1980.

In 1971, the IRA's Post Office Tower bomb launched their mainland bombing campaign, which would predominantly target London. The year 1979 saw both the assassination of the Queen's uncle, Earl Mountbatten, and Northern Ireland's Secretary of State, Airey Neave MP, who was killed outside the House of Commons. In the intervening years, there were IRA bombs at stations, shopping centres, clubs and hotels. Several people were killed, many more injured. Arguably, the most memorable IRA-related event was in Northern Ireland itself. On 30 January 1972, later known as 'Bloody Sunday', thirteen unarmed civil rights protestors and bystanders were shot and killed by British soldiers in Derry (a fourteenth victim died of his injuries several months later). It took many years and several inquiries to establish the soldiers' guilt. The Saville Inquiry began in 1998, with its condemning report finally produced in 2010.

The 1970s brought extremes of weather. 'Snow Stops Play' declared a June 1975 headline after the Lancashire/Derbyshire cricket match at Buxton was abandoned. The warmest summer since 1947 followed, with the 'Hampstead Storm' hitting north-west London in August, closing four mainline railway stations and flooding part of the underground network. However, it was the 1976 heatwave, from June until the end of August, that remains in the collective memory. During that period, the temperature reached 25°C on sixty-two days. People recalled 'a plague of ladybirds' and pubs running out of beer. Tar softened, pavements cracked, even vinyl records melted. Hosepipes were banned, standpipes appeared on street corners. A significant number of house-buyers avoided houses built in 1976, fearing subsidence. Happier memories included sunbathing, sitting in haystacks and having water fights. MP Denis Howell became Minister for Drought, and then later Minister of Floods, when the rains finally came.

Environmental concerns over nuclear power and the burgeoning world population continued. The term 'green' appeared, alongside

Queensgate, Huddersfield, 1970. This area was redeveloped in 1970 with a new market hall and multi-storey car park (on the left).

the Ecology Party. *The Ecologist* magazine attracted attention with a special 1972 issue, entitled *Blue-print For Survival*. E. F. Schumacher's 1973 best-seller, *Small Is Beautiful*, fiercely opposed mounting consumption. Millions of television viewers were introduced to 'self-sufficiency' through BBC 1's *The Good Life* (1975–78), set in middle-class Surrey, where Tom and Barbara Good tried to 'grow their own' and survive without money. In 1975, Britain's first waste-recycling centre opened in Huddersfield, with a £2 million modern incinerator.

The Queen's Silver Jubilee year culminated on 6 June 1977, with street parties across Britain. Derby was awarded city status and, in addition to London Underground's new Jubilee line, Jubilee Gardens were created on the South Bank of the Thames. Support for the Royal Family was thought to have declined, yet millions marked the anniversary of the Coronation. Huge crowds on London's Mall, a sea of Union flags, sang the National Anthem. A significant minority shunned the occasion. Anti-royalist protests were headed by punk group the Sex Pistols, with their anarchic top-selling single, 'God Save The Queen', but, for the majority of Britons, the Jubilee celebrations formed a welcome diversion from economic ills.

Men from the village of Dry Drayton, Cambridgeshire, celebrating the Queen's Jubilee, 6 June 1977.

Shopping and Fashion

D URING THE 1970s, notable developments in retailing led to changes in the nation's shopping habits. In cities and large towns, supermarket chains, and even hypermarkets, mushroomed. People shopped less frequently, and for a greater range of items, which were increasingly available in one large store. These changes threatened the livelihood of small independent shopkeepers. The growth of car ownership and home freezers also encouraged shopping weekly, rather than the traditional daily trek to the local corner shop. The spiralling cost of food and other products, arguably exacerbated by the introduction of decimalisation in 1971, resulted for some in falling living standards. At the same time, for many, shopping for clothes and accessories – supplied by a fast-growing and wide-ranging British fashion industry – became a leisure pursuit.

Food shopping took on a different meaning in the 1970s as larger supermarkets and self-service superstores appeared on the outskirts of towns. Tesco adopted a new image; Sir Terry Leahy, later Chief Executive, recalled that previously people 'only used Tesco for cheap, dented tins', preferring Sainsbury's or Waitrose 'for their main shop'. By the late 1970s, abandoning its 'pile it high sell it cheap' philosophy, Tesco closed five hundred unprofitable shops, and developed large out-of-town stores, often with Esso petrol stations. Sainsbury's responded by slashing prices and opening their SavaCentre hypermarket chain.

Other supermarkets also grew – Waitrose in southern England, Morrisons in the north. Co-operatives continued to be popular in northern industrial areas, London and in Scotland, where Safeway also flourished. Smaller Scottish chains, like William Low, doubled in size. Marks & Spencer (M&S), the first British retailer to introduce 'sell by' dates on food to guarantee freshness, began to stock convenience foods.

Freezing revolutionised food shopping. New specialist freezer shops encouraged bulk-buying, urging 'Beat inflation, buy now!' Iceland's

Opposite: David Bowie, innovative 1970s rock musician, performing as his alter ego, Ziggy Stardust in 1973.

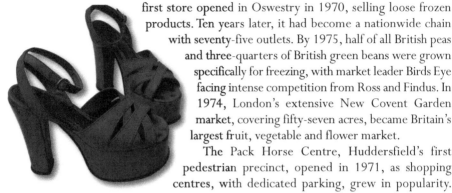

first store opened in Oswestry in 1970, selling loose frozen products. Ten years later, it had become a nationwide chain with seventy-five outlets. By 1975, half of all British peas and three-quarters of British green beans were grown specifically for freezing, with market leader Birds Eye facing intense competition from Ross and Findus. In 1974, London's extensive New Covent Garden market, covering fifty-seven acres, became Britain's largest fruit, vegetable and flower market.

The Pack Horse Centre, Huddersfield's first pedestrian precinct, opened in 1971, as shopping centres, with dedicated parking, grew in popularity. Britain's first 'stand-alone' shopping centre opened in 1976 at London's Brent Cross, followed by many more, including Manchester's Arndale (1979). These new shopping facilities were popular, but not always visually attractive; St James Centre was later voted 'Edinburgh's ugliest building'. Smaller suburban and town precincts also grew.

Typical women's high platform shoes.

Two children completing a school survey outside a fish shop in a small Cambridge shopping precinct, c. 1979.

Independent stores were badly affected by the new shopping trends, their numbers falling by almost two-thirds between 1961 and 1979. Sainsbury's closed many of its small high-street shops, where shoppers had queued separately at different counters. Village shops were also unable to compete. After 1974, over 40 per cent of Dorset and Nottinghamshire villages had no shop. Those with post offices hung on longer, as in Dry Drayton, Cambridgeshire, where the village shop-cum-post office remained open throughout the decade, selling everything from 'welly boots to whisky'. Some small stores, and new Indian 'takeaway' outlets, were kept open by immigrant Asian families who worked long hours serving their local communities.

Changes in shopping habits hit the poor who were already facing inflationary prices. Those without cars were frequently unable to take advantage of the cheaper supermarkets, and so were forced to resort to the fast-disappearing local shops where prices tended to be higher. Home catalogue shopping, with weekly payments, was one possible answer for those on lower incomes. Glossy catalogues – the top seller was Littlewoods – offered dreams of a better lifestyle. In 1979, Freemans introduced an agents' telephone ordering service; other successful firms included Great Universal and Ace.

Additionally, reward stamps, exchangeable for gifts, were still popular in the early 1970s. Green Shield stamps, used by Tesco, were the most well known. In 1976, top gifts, that could take years to obtain, included a Creda cooker: 115 books of stamps; a Hotpoint automatic washing machine: 185; or a Phillips colour television: 375. BOAC accepted Green Shield stamps in full or part-payment for flights; even cars were available, 'just ask for a quotation'. Stamp use declined as customers realised they paid for gifts through higher shop prices. Sainsbury's, John Lewis, Marks & Spencer and WH Smith had always opposed stamps. By the late 1970s, Tesco had also discontinued their use.

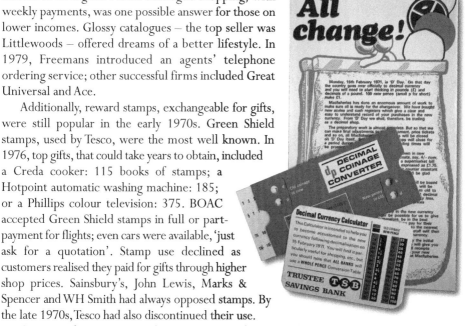

On 15 February 1971, the United Kingdom switched to a decimalised currency, which was initially controversial. Despite extensive marketing – in 1970, the Scottish company, Burroughs, took a decimal display round secondary schools – many thought

Britain moved from imperial to decimal currency on 15 February 1971.

Aerial view of Dry Drayton village, showing the general village shop-cum-post office, c. 1970s.

Formality and informality: three generations of the Shepherd family in Swanage, c. 1978. While older generations continued to wear traditional clothing, younger people adopted new fashions and fabrics.

the 'new money' rounded prices up. 'We're here to help' headlined the *Daily Mirror*, advertising 'price watch' phone numbers. Both customers and shopkeepers found the new money confusing. In Papworth, Cambridgeshire, for some time after the switchover, people took their change from 'a pot of new money near the till'.

While many people still dressed conservatively, the 1970s are remembered for plentiful, often outrageous fashions. Expensive London fashion shops included Biba (opened 1973), in Kensington High Street, on the old Derry & Toms' site, where one bride bought 'a big floppy straw going-away hat'. In Cambridge, Snob did brisk business in Market Square while Barneys on the cosmopolitan Mill Road provided a cheaper popular local outlet. A Barneys' advertisement in 1973 featured 1920s-style trousers for men, with puffed sleeves back 'in' for women. Edinburgh's booming department store, Patrick Thomson's, ('PTs'), had a large fashion-conscious clientele in the early 1970s; in the Scottish Borders many textile and knitwear factories had on-site shops selling quality knitwear, with seconds or range ends for the less affluent. There was an overall growth in the use of polyester fabrics for everyday wear.

An iconic young 1970s look – long hair, wide lapels, flares and high-wedge footwear – was common to many from both sexes. Platform shoes, often with 5–10cm thick soles, became an indelible image. But the decade sported many other fashion styles. For women, the early 1970s still featured the mini skirt, but also 'midi' and 'maxi' lengths, often in bold patterns. Hot pants and short dungarees, 'pedal pushers', were all the rage from 1971; pop sox and textured tights from the mid-1970s, also hard wooden Scholl exercise sandals that 'killed your feet until you got used to them'.

Wedding dresses were generally long, especially for church ceremonies. A group of women, who all married in 1972, recalled their long, fashionable, Laura Ashley wedding dresses; only one, who had a register office wedding, opted for a lace mini. Another hired wedding dress, veil, tiara and shoes for £35 from Youngs, near Oxford Street. Men went to dinner parties in suits; women in long dresses, or long skirts topped with frilly blouses. British fashion designer, Norman

Hartnell, reviewing the Great Universal's catalogue in 1973, noted 'glittery evening wear trimmings'. Party makeup was influenced in 1972 by the flamboyant 'glam and glitter' makeup worn by David Bowie's androgynous alter ego, Ziggy Stardust.

For the 'daytime woman', natural-looking makeup was preferred. A light touch of blusher replaced old-fashioned rouge, but 'spit and brush' hard mascara from a tin was still used. Hair was generally long; in 1971, actress Susan Penhaligon, the 'British Brigitte Bardot', had a sought-after look with long blonde hair, big eyes and healthy glowing skin. In 1974, fashion icon Mary Quant launched cosmetics and perfumes. Two years later, 'inspired by nature', Anita Roddick opened the first The Body Shop in Brighton; its unusual name, however, initially incurred objections from a local undertaker.

Foreign holidays encouraged ethnic clothing: ponchos, long afghan coats, ankle-length floral/patchwork dresses and tie-dye shirts. Women's swimwear at the start of the decade was still modest. At the Miss World 1970 finals in London's Royal Albert Hall – famously interrupted by feminist activists throwing flour bombs – all the contestants wore one-piece costumes.

For men, flared trousers with turn-ups and cheesecloth shirts were later replaced for many younger men by drainpipe jeans and ripped

Wedding guests in 1973, showing an eclectic range of contemporary fashions: long dress, mini skirts, beards and moustaches, and wide ties.

Snappy dresser: car salesman Graham Lovelock sports trendy long hair, wide 'kipper' tie and three-piece suit, Teignmouth, Devon, c. 1970s.

T-shirts. Garishly coloured three-piece suits became fashionable. Long hair, sideburns, beards and moustaches were increasingly common. Young black men wore afro hairstyles throughout the decade. The range of men's toiletries expanded. Boxer Henry Cooper famously advertised Brut products; he was later given so much Brut he had to stack it in his garage.

The age at which boys should wear long trousers became a social issue, even discussed in the press. Later in the decade, with the influx of jeans, boys' short trousers virtually disappeared. Hardwearing 'fur'-lined parka jackets with hoods were common, worn by most schoolchildren. Disco style, featuring bright, easy-to-wear clothing, hit the youth market in the late 1970s, influenced by the blockbuster 1977 film, *Saturday Night Fever*, starring John Travolta. 'Boob tubes' appeared from 1979, also mules and ankle-strap shoes, reminiscent of the 1940s. Mary Quant's fashion-conscious Daisy doll for little girls sported cutting-edge design from 1973, with, at different times, 'stretch polyester T-shirts, fake "fun fur", gypsy-style dresses and boiler suits'.

From the mid-1970s, punk urban street culture invaded fashion, shocking established norms. Old clothes were drastically altered, with the addition of safety pins, razor blades and chains. Body-piercing jewellery, memorably rows of three ear studs, spiked dog collars and tattoos, aided the image, plus heavy Doc Martens footwear. Hair was frequently spiked, using gelatine, hairspray and PVA glue.

Two British designers in particular adapted and promoted punk clothing. Vivienne Westwood, 'messianic about punk', sold fetish leather and rubber clothing in a boutique she ran with her boyfriend, Malcolm McLaren (later manager of the Sex Pistols). The shop, which opened in 1971, was named 'SEX' between 1974 and 1976, and stocked designs by Westwood and McLaren alongside fetish wear. By 1977, Zandra Rhodes incorporated punk into her collections, with expensive, up-market versions. 'Anarchic and aggressive', punk remained an important face of colourful 1970s fashion.

FOOD AND DRINK

IN THE 1970S, BRITONS GENERALLY enjoyed a greater variety and quantity of food and drink than previously, due to developments in modern technology, mechanisation and production. The range of available products widened. According to the Office of National Statistics 1970 Report, over a fifth of domestic expenditure went on food and non-alcoholic drinks, representing a lower percentage of family budgets than in previous decades. Greater disposable income therefore led to rising living standards. In addition, Britain's decision to join the EEC in 1973 had a lasting impact on the supply and provision of foodstuffs. Increasingly more imports came from Europe than the Commonwealth; the post-war era of cheap 'Empire' food, such as New Zealand lamb, was over.

The advent of the freezer in British homes changed the nation's diet irrevocably. The 1970s also witnessed a massive rise in the consumption of heavily promoted convenience and fast foods, resulting in less home cooking. However, a growing minority of Britons discovered health foods. Continental holidays introduced the British nation to 'foreign foods' and drinking wine with meals. Coffee began to challenge tea as the country's favourite beverage. In general, increased leisure time resulted in more entertaining with an inevitable rise in alcohol consumption.

From time to time, world trade fluctuations, such as the 1974 sugar crisis, brought increased prices and temporary

Biba Food Hall poster, Knightsbridge London, late 1970s. Uniquely, the food hall contained units designed like the product they were selling, e.g. dog food was sold from a dog-shaped section.

food shortages. A 1976 drought and potato blight resulted in a greater consumption of rice and pasta. Panic buying and bread rationing followed the 1978 national bakers' strike; only a minority of people made their own bread.

Overall, modern technology and mechanisation led to increased production. The volume of milk produced, and consumed, soared. A typical hen laid twice as many eggs than its predecessor in the 1950s. One shopper recalled buying 'cheese, bread, butter, potatoes, vegetables, a chicken and more' for five pounds in 1973. The same year, London's Fortnum & Mason reported booming sales of *foie gras* to its wealthy clientele.

Most homes had a refrigerator and many soon had freezers; one in ten households by 1974, two in five by 1979. Large chest models were frequently housed in garages, filled with fish fingers, chips, peas or 'half a cow to share with neighbours'. Out-of-season foods became available all year round. The *Home and Freezer Digest*, appearing in 1973, declared, 'It's not just what the freezer can do for you but what the freezer frees you to do'. Sales of ice cream rose as it became a regular dessert instead of an occasional treat. Cookery books included puddings that could only be made using a freezer. 'The Frozen Limit' episode of ITV's *Bless This House* (1976) saw Sid (veteran actor Sid James) reluctantly persuaded by his wife to purchase a freezer. Expensive domestic microwaves were available by the end of the decade, costing between £150 and £400, but public concerns over cost and radioactivity affected sales.

From 1970, 'convenience foods' increasingly replaced home cooking. In 1971, the *Huddersfield Daily Examiner*'s 'favourite recipe competition' found most people used canned, rather than fresh vegetables. Ange in *Abigail's Party* enthusiastically described her 'pilchard curry', made with tinned pilchards in tomato sauce (available in new, ring-pull cans). Delia Smith's first cookery book, *How To Cheat At Cooking* (1971) and her 1973 *Family Fare* television series, tried, unsuccessfully, to return the nation to home-cooked food.

Sales of 'convenient' sliced white bread in plastic bags soared. Instant mashed potato, Smash, became popular after a memorable 1974 television advertisement, later voted 'TV Advert of the

Pot Noodle, c. 1970s. Boiling water added to dried noodles and vegetables created an 'instant' meal. Convenience foods were increasingly popular during the 1970s.

Century', portrayed Martians laughing at 'earthlings' peeling, cooking and mashing potatoes. 'Boil-in-the-bag' fish appeared; chicken Kiev, marketed by M&S, became a bestselling 'instant' meal. Pot Noodle and Snack Pots competed with hot school dinners, especially from 1979 when there was no longer a legal requirement for local authorities to provide school meals.

People ate out more. By 1979, nearly a million firms provided employees with daily luncheon vouchers as part of their remuneration. Originating from the USA, fast food and 'takeaway' outlets spread in Britain, serving fried chicken, pizzas and hamburgers. Kentucky Fried Chicken and Pizza Hut were followed by the first McDonald's in Woolwich in 1974; two years later, McDonald's was running regular television and cinema advertisements. By 1976, the phrase 'junk food' had entered the British language.

Concerns over food safety and suitability attracted little attention until late in the decade, the consensus throughout much

'Boil-in-the-bag' became a popular way to prepare convenience foods, c. 1970s.

margarine
butter
dripping
lard and cooking fats
solid vegetable oils
shredded suet

By 27 August 1979 all prepacked margarine and butter will be sold in metric. The other fats will follow by 31 December 1979 and shredded suet by 29 September 1980.

Examples of the new pack sizes:
500 g replacing 1 lb (or 454 g)
250 g replacing 8 oz (or 227 g)
125 g replacing 4 oz (or 113 g)
shredded suet will be available from most shops only in 250 g packs.

These metric weights are just over ten per cent more than those they replace. So the new packs may cost more but they will go further.

shopping in metric 1979

MARGARINE · BUTTER · FATS · TEA & TEABAGS

A leaflet listing common foods to be sold in metric weights from 27 August 1979. Tea and sugar were highlighted, also many popular 1970s 'fats' products.

Birthday party tea for the Parry twins in 1977, with fairy cakes, jam tarts, and the 'grown-up' treat of cheese on sticks (not shown).

of the 1970s being that food was generally safe. A 1973 Setlers indigestion tablets advertisement suggested consumers always knew when they 'ate something they shouldn't'. A 1979 leaflet introducing metric measures highlighted the decade's most common products, which in addition to tea and sugar included several 'fats' products.

Advertising new foods became big business. Manufacturers boosted sales by targeting children: Mr Men appeared on yoghurt pots; Lyons' cakes featured characters from TV favourites *The Wombles* and *The Magic Roundabout*. Instant Angel Delight mousse joined traditional strawberry jelly at children's parties. Fizzy drinks, in newly marketed plastic bottles, registered increased sales, despite warnings of tooth decay and hyperactivity in children. When Value Added Tax replaced Purchase Tax, on 1 April 1973, ice cream and chocolate were exempt; by 9 April, Cadbury's were advertising price reductions on a hundred chocolate lines. Popular new 1970s sweets included Yorkie and Lion Bar (1976) and Twix (1979).

Soft drinks advertisements won awards. R. White's 1973 advertisement, the 'Secret Lemonade Drinker', was long remembered; the singer was Elvis Costello's father, Ross

MacManus, with his son providing backing vocals. *I'd Like To Teach The World To Sing* by The New Seekers began as a 1971 jingle, later becoming a pop-song in its own right and 'the face of Coca-Cola' for years to come.

Despite the growth of convenience foods, health foods grew in popularity, with a boom in diet drinks and fat-free yoghurt. More people drank fruit juices, from new lightweight plastic or

Sam Shepherd, lorry driver, 'fries up' by the roadside, *c.* 1979.

British comedian Peter Cook, his wife, Judy Huxtable, comedy partner Dudley Moore and Moore's girlfriend Alys Hastings, celebrate the new year with wine, 1 January 1973. Peter Cook and Dudley Moore's hugely successful 1960s partnership continued into the early 1970s.

cardboard containers. Some breakfast cereals were 'organically grown', with Weetabix's first 'Swiss-style muesli' marketed in 1971. The *Whole Earth Cook Book* (1972) advertised 'natural foods'. By the end of the decade, although red meat was still popular, chicken had begun to replace beef as the nation's preferred Sunday roast; bacon and eggs, however, remained the favourite breakfast choice.

Alongside the growth of environmental concerns, more people became vegetarians. The Vegetarian Society campaigns began, with their new, later famous, seedling logo. Soya mince appeared in 1972. Popular vegetarian classics included stuffed peppers, nut roasts and cheese fondue. However, the 1970s witnessed a decline in home-grown vegetables as thousands of allotments were sold. *The Good Life* prompted some householders to cultivate their own food; more viewers, however, probably identified with the Goods' well-heeled conventional shop-using neighbours, Margo and Jerry Leadbetter.

Holidays abroad stimulated a taste for foreign food. As the decade wore on, Sainsbury's reported increased sales of fresh pasta and extra-virgin olive oil, as well as German bio-yoghurt, French bread and American ice cream. Paella was a reminder of the Costa Brava.

'Galloping Gourmet' TV chef, Graham Kerr, featured continental staples, garlic and avocados; garlic crushers became available in Habitat. In 1978 French Brie and Camembert advertisements asked, 'Why wait for a dinner party to enjoy them?' Famous Indian actress and cookery writer, Madhur Jaffrey, introduced Indian food to British kitchens, presaging its later meteoric rise in popularity. By 1976, Chinese takeaways outnumbered fish-and-chip shops.

Tea remained the national drink as tea-bags replaced loose tea. 'It's those little perforations that make all the difference' sang a Tetley advertisement; competitor Typhoo ran a 'better flavour, money saver' campaign. By 1979, the cost of a 'cuppa' rose when the price of milk increased by 10 per cent. Unigate's 1976 'milk thief' television advertisement, featuring famous personalities Barbara Windsor and Rod Hull, was hugely successful, with associated merchandise (mugs, milk bottles, straws) later becoming collectable.

Meanwhile, coffee grew in popularity. Most households had jars of 'instant', with Nescafé Gold Blend the posh choice. Aficionados recall classy coffee percolators, with specialist shops selling ground coffee. Upwardly mobile suburbanites bought cafetières and coffee beans to grind at home. One 1970s schoolgirl remembers trying coffee 'just in case a boy asked me out for one'.

Watneys' large Party Seven cans of beer were all the rage, c. 1970s.

Dinner-party recipes of the 1970s have joined food folklore: prawn cocktail, then chicken chasseur, steak or gammon and pineapple, followed by Black Forest gateau, sherry trifle or baked Alaska. Buffet food in *Abigail's Party* included cheese straws, cocktail sausages and olives for the trendy. Wine drinking, cheaper after Britain joined the EEC, became more usual; 'up-market Chablis' featured in BBC TV's *Fawlty Towers'* gourmet evening. Cocktails, also whisky and soda (from an essential Sparklets Soda Syphon), were increasingly chosen. In *Abigail's Party*, the guests drank Bacardi and Coke, or gin and tonic – always with ice and lemon. Martini sold well 'anytime, any place, anywhere'. The popularity of keg bitters like Whitbread's Trophy, 'the pint that thinks it's a quart', declined as CAMRA, the Campaign For Real Ale, grew apace. For many, the 1970s are remembered as 'the party-time decade'.

'I wanted
a low tar cigaret
I could taste
—now I've found

JOHN PLAYER
KING SIZE

LOW TAR · LOW TAR · LOW TAR

JOHN PLAYER
KING SIZE

EXTRA MILD

JOHN PLAYER
KING SIZE EXTRA MILD

LOW TAR As defined in H.M. Government Tables

H.M. Government Health Departments' WARNING:
CIGARETTES CAN SERIOUSLY DAMAGE YOUR HEALTH

HEALTH

THE FIRST MAJOR CHANGES in the administration of the thirty-year-old National Health Service (NHS) occurred in the 1970s. As the cost of running the health service escalated, the private sector increasingly competed for patients, while nurses were dissatisfied with their pay and status. Nonetheless, the decade saw significant medical advances, most notably progress in some cancer treatments and the successful pioneering concept and development of *in vitro* fertilisation (IVF), leading to the birth of the world's first 'test tube' baby.

The year 1974 saw major NHS re-organisation, introducing a new three-tiered administrative structure aimed at rationalising an ever-expanding service. Primary care was to be provided by general practitioners (GPs), secondary care by regional hospitals. Local area health authorities would cater for a range of services, including ambulance, child and welfare services, answerable in turn to regional health authorities, themselves accountable to the minister of health. The new structure was soon criticised as complicated and top-heavy.

The changes resulted in considerable disruption and many small hospital closures, while some major hospitals, like Addenbrooke's in Cambridge, expanded. London's Royal Free Hospital relocated to larger premises in Hampstead. Leeds' St James's Hospital, 'Jimmy's', became a university hospital from 1970, following the expansion of the Leeds Medical School. Oxford's John Radcliffe Hospital opened in 1972, and was extended by 1979.

By 1970, although the NHS was still 'free at the point of need', many Britons increasingly purchased private health care. An ideological battle developed over the treatment of private patients under the NHS with one side arguing that private and public health care could co-exist and flourish, the other that private insurance schemes undermined the state health service, competing for scarce resources. Yet, by 1979, three-quarters of all 'pay-beds' remained, as private health care expanded, rather than shrank. BUPA, and other

Opposite: A John Player advert, c. 1979. Many women considered 'low tar' cigarettes healthier. John Player sponsored the Formula One Lotus motor racing team; from 1972, Lotus drivers wore John Player Special colours of black and gold.

'Angry and frustrated' nurses, Addenbrooke's Hospital, c. 1979. 'We have been taken for granted for too long.' Nationwide, nurses complained about a low 1979 pay offer.

Aerial view of Addenbrooke's Hospital, late 1970s. In 1976, the hospital moved from its original central Cambridge site to larger premises on the city outskirts, becoming a renowned teaching hospital. Its tall chimney became a familiar sight for local commuters arriving at Cambridge railway station.

private hospitals, offered faster treatment to those who had no philosophical objections and who could pay. Within the NHS, the growing drugs bill necessitated prescription charges, equating to 20p per item by 1971, more than doubling by 1979, to 45p. Concerns over spiralling costs led to the creation of 'Friends' associations, raising money for individual hospitals to buy equipment.

The 1970 Briggs Committee recommendations for improvements to nurses' professional education were later incorporated into the 1979 Nurses, Midwives and Health Visitors Act. However, nurses' main concern in the 1970s was the level of pay. A senior nurse recalled the 1970s as an era of 'pay-beds and strikes', when nurses felt undervalued and underpaid. A strike in 1972 was followed two years later by nurses marching on Downing Street, resulting in an independent inquiry and a long-overdue 30 per cent pay rise. Yet, in a decade when some hospital facilities were improving, and Manchester University appointed the first ever professor of nursing, the Royal College of Nursing felt compelled to become a trade union in 1977 to fight for nurses' rights. By 1979, nurses were again very dissatisfied with their pay.

In the maternity sector, in a departure from the norm, some mothers opted for drug-free 'natural childbirth' and by the early 1970s, the National Childbirth Trust had thirty-seven branches, providing information about pregnancy and birth, and antenatal classes. The 'homebirth' movement similarly grew, lobbying for more babies to be born at home. The sexual revolution of the 1960s and 1970s unfortunately also led to a huge rise in unwanted pregnancies and, from 1967, legal abortions.

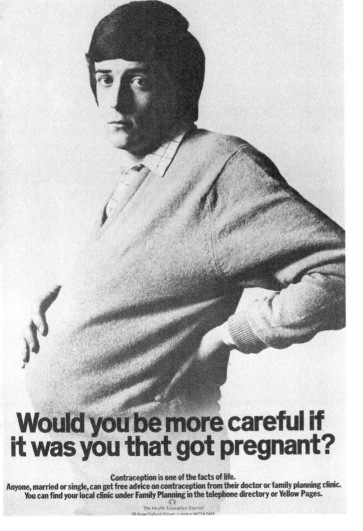

Would you be more careful if it was you that got pregnant?

Contraception is one of the facts of life.
Anyone, married or single, can get free advice on contraception from their doctor or family planning clinic.
You can find your local clinic under Family Planning in the telephone directory or Yellow Pages.

The Health Education Council
78 New Oxford Street, London WC1A 1AH

Attempts to instil a more mature male approach towards contraception were captured in this iconic 1975 Health Education Council poster.

A St Thomas' Hospital child patient card, c. 1970s. 'Every morning the nurses, in their complicated folded hats, knelt in a circle for morning prayers. Sister wore a very elaborate high pleated hat with an enormous bow under her chin.'

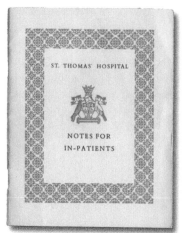

Growing interest in child welfare saw the launch of the British Births Survey (later British Cohort Study), collecting data about nearly eighteen thousand babies born between 5 and 11 April 1970. Initially concerned just with neo-natal mortality rates, the survey later developed into a comprehensive study of children's health. By 1975, it incorporated physical and educational development; by 1980, social development was included. Elsewhere, student health was studied, most notably the impact of psychological anxiety on academic performance.

Concern over children's health grew during the decade. Infant welfare milk was controversially abolished in 1970. A year later, Education Secretary, Margaret Thatcher, was widely criticized for abolishing free school milk for over-sevens, despite warnings of possible detrimental health effects. It earned her the perennial nickname, 'Milk Snatcher'. Child tooth decay was another concern. Although fluoride in toothpaste was already reducing damage, and lowering NHS dental costs, mass fluoridation was opposed by many who feared serious health consequences; only a few local authorities added fluoride to their water supply. The whooping-cough vaccine was also contentious as severe brain injury had occurred in a small number of cases. However, as incidences of the disease were declining, risk comparisons suggested that for most healthy children the vaccine dangers exceeded those of the disease itself. Rates of childhood asthma and hay fever, leading to increased hospital admissions, rose dramatically in the 1970s, especially during the hot summer of 1976.

Industrial action interrupted health provision at both ends of the decade. Power-station workers took action in December 1970, esulting in cancellations, or operations by candlelight. Standby ;enerators were used to keep premature babies alive and ensure safe 'lood storage. In 1972, the ongoing miners' strike led to a rota of 'lectricity cuts, although areas around hospitals were protected.)uring the 1978–79 'winter of discontent', however, many hospitals vere affected by striking public-sector hospital workers. At London's Westminster Hospital in January 1979, 'piles of dirty linen filled the :orridors'. During this time, cabinet minister David Ennals had an)peration at the hospital, but, by 30 January, no new patients could be idmitted. Millions listening to Radio 2's Jimmy Young show in early 1979 heard Margaret Thatcher accuse unions of 'confronting the sick', is cancer patients were sent home and the dead remained unburied. Jnion members, however, many of whom had not been on strike)efore, believed passionately that they were justified and the dispute :ontinued.

In an ageing population, although long-term geriatric and)sychiatric wards still existed, more elderly people remained in the :ommunity, living in nursing homes. From 1972, MIND (previously National Association for Mental Health) began lobbying, focusing on iousing needs, better rehabilitation and, by 1979, the specific needs

'Don't do drugs!' Brentwood schoolboys listen to a detective inspector warn about the dangers of drug taking, January 1970.

of the elderly mentally infirm. *Better Services for the Mentally Ill* (1975) urged more integration between the voluntary sector and NHS, but, at a time of recession, it had limited impact. From 1977, health authorities could transfer money to support local authority services and by the end of the decade, plans for an Alzheimer's Society were under way.

The first British Medical Association report on smoking in 1971 led to health warnings on cigarette packets which, coupled with the growth of the anti-smoking lobby, highlighted the risks. With about twenty-five popular brands, cigarettes brought huge financial profits to the tobacco industry. Some smokers switched to so-called 'milder' brands; a 1972 Benson & Hedges 'milder' Silk Cut advertisement claimed annual sales had 'quadrupled'. Smoking among men peaked in 1973/74, with over a quarter of British men classed as heavy smokers. Thereafter the number of male smokers declined, but an increase in the number of women smoking led to more incidences of lung cancer in women.

Drug addiction became a major concern by the early 1970s, with LSD regularly taken at clubs and festivals. Although the 1971 Misuse of Drugs Act classed cannabis as less dangerous than heroin, the fear in the general populace of progression from soft to hard drugs grew. By 1979, there were significantly more heroin addicts than at the start of the decade.

Arguably the greatest treatment disaster in the history of the NHS occurred in the late 1970s when contaminated blood products produced by certain pharmaceutical companies inadvertently infected thousands of haemophiliacs with deadly viruses such as HIV and Hepatitis C. This catastrophic error caused both individual tragedies and a major public-health problem.

Medical progress led to technological advances such as computerised tomography (CT) scans for X-raying soft brain tissues from 1972 and the development of nuclear magnetic resonance (NMR) scanners. The use of endoscopies, kidney dialysis and intensive care units grew. Endorphins, the body's natural painkillers, were discovered in the brain in 1975. The year 1979 saw two British firsts – a successful British bone-marrow transplant on a child at Great Ormond Street Hospital, and a successful British heart transplant at Papworth Hospital, an increasingly famous centre for heart surgery.

There was welcome progress in the battle against cancer. The NHS, with help from a major cancer charity, created five new oncology research units. Mortality rates for Hodgkin's lymphoma fell by a third, testicular cancer by a quarter, while breast cancer, male

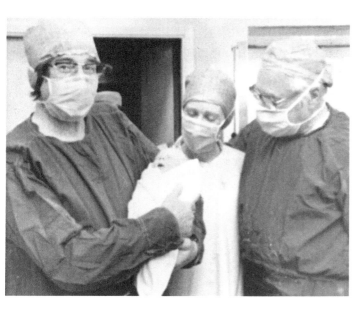

Dr Robert Edwards, holding Louise Brown, the world's first IVF baby, with gynaecologist Mr Patrick Steptoe, at Oldham General Hospital on 25 July 1978.

lung cancer and bowel cancer rates (one in twenty-nine men; one in twenty-six women) remained static. The year 1975 saw the first Macmillan cancer care unit and a specifically trained Macmillan nurse to care for the terminally ill. By 1979, there were ten such nurses, although funded by charitable donations, not the NHS. The decade also saw the growth of the Hospice movement, founded in 1967 by Cicely Saunders.

Undoubtedly, the decade's most notable medical advance was the development of the *in vitro* ('in glass') method of fertilising an egg outside the human body, then reintroducing it into the mother's womb. Ten years of pioneering work by Cambridge physiologist Dr Robert Edwards (Nobel prize 2010; knighted 2011) and Mr Patrick Steptoe, gynaecological surgeon, led to the birth of the world's first 'test tube' baby, Louise Brown, at Oldham, Lancashire in 1978. Louise's birth made medical history, bringing new hope for many couples who experienced difficulty conceiving. However, the procedure raised some profound ethical issues.

By the end of the decade, NHS costs were rising year on year. 'Meditate and save the NHS millions' said a 1978 *Times* headline, citing a group of doctors who advocated meditation instead of sedatives. Nonetheless, a 1978 London conference celebrated the thirtieth anniversary of a national health service that, despite its problems, remained the envy of the world.

EDUCATION AND SOCIAL SERVICES

THROUGHOUT THE 1970s, education was a subject of keen public interest, often dominating the news, with controversies over the primary-school curriculum, and selective grammar schools versus non-selective comprehensives. The decade also witnessed the expansion of higher education, particularly the creation of new universities and polytechnics. There were also significant changes, with a contraction in numbers, in initial teacher training. The provision of social services became more challenging, with increasing pressure on the state to provide better care for society's vulnerable groups, including the young, the aged and the unemployed.

Primary education was heavily influenced by the child-centred 1967 Plowden Report; by the 1970s, most primary schools had adopted its recommendations. Primary-school staff had considerable autonomy. Often, only physical-education lessons were timetabled, leaving teachers free to determine curriculum content and organisation. Some schools became noted for particular emphases. Prior Weston, in London's Barbican, a flagship 'Plowden primary school' under its progressive headteacher, Henry Pluckrose, became renowned for creativity and its child-centred curriculum.

In 1971, only a fifth of under-fives received nursery education. Many nurseries were privately run. Plowden's aims to achieve state provision for most four-year-olds in England within a decade were adopted in the 1972 White Paper, *A Framework For Expansion*, but implementation took much longer. *Before Five*, promoting Scottish nursery education, resulted in the far quicker establishment of nursery classes in Scotland's primary schools.

Plowden's focus on the 'child at the centre of the curriculum' was criticised by some as trendy and irresponsible, as was the phasing out of corporal punishment in most primary schools in the early 1970s. Five right-wing Black Papers, 1969 to 1977 (authors C. B. Cox, A. E. Dyson, Rhodes Boyson), believed progressive methods resulted in 'educational

Opposite: Pupils in the science laboratory at Hackney Downs Comprehensive School, c. 1970.

decline'. Their argument was fuelled by the 1974 'William Tyndale affair', when the radical head of an Islington primary school and some of his staff were dismissed by the Inner London Education Authority (ILEA) for poor teaching, leading to the two-year Auld public inquiry. The London borough of Islington was also renowned for Highbury Grove Comprehensive, run like a traditional grammar by its well-known head teacher, Rhodes Boyson – Black Paper author, later Conservative MP and government minister. At the other end of the borough, the radical, egalitarian, all-age White Lion Free School provided an alternative education, espousing 'freedom and democracy'.

In a 1976 keynote speech at Ruskin College, Oxford, Prime Minister James Callaghan opened a 'Great Debate' on education, initiating discussion on a possible compulsory 'core curriculum' and a return to the norms and standards of traditional education. Major reports supported a need for change. The Bullock Report on English teaching (1975) urged a greater emphasis on reading, also on nurturing pupils with English as a second language. A 1976 Lancaster University paper, on teaching styles and pupils' progress, decried liberal methods and an important 1978 Primary Inspectors' report criticised current teaching styles and attainment. The declining birth rate in the 1970s in turn led to falling school rolls, resulting in some school closures.

By the 1970s, the national move towards comprehensive education had progressed too far to be halted. By 1975, most local education authorities (LEAs) had adopted a non-selective system; grammar schools either amalgamated with local secondary moderns, or closed. Only a small number of LEAs, like Kent and Dorset, retained grammars. Between 1970 and 1974, the percentage of children

Keeping up old traditions: maypole dancing at Blaise Primary School, Bristol, 1976.

Christmas concert at St Albans, a private nursery school in High Barnet, Hertfordshire, 1973.

attending comprehensives almost doubled, to 62 per cent. Opinions were polarised. *Panorama* produced 'fly on the wall' footage of Ealing's Faraday High School in 1977, revealing scenes of chaotic indiscipline. Comprehensive schools advocate, ILEA council leader Ashley Bramall, countered with examples of good schools. The ILEA was also one of the first authorities to abolish corporal punishment in all its secondary schools in 1973, years before a national ban.

Economic downturns resulted in an increasing number of unemployed school leavers, many of whom lacked vocational training. LEAs were encouraged to organise work experience for fifteen- to sixteen-year-olds to prepare them for the 'world of work' and, in 1973, the school leaving age finally rose to sixteen. By 1978, the new single General Certificate of Secondary Education had replaced 'Ordinary level' and Certificate of Secondary Education exams. The curriculum was becoming less gender-based; from 1972, Impington Village College, a Cambridgeshire comprehensive, encouraged boys to study needlework and textiles.

The 1970s was an important decade for special education. A 1970 Act entitled all children to education, ending the use of the term 'ineducable'. The *Fit for the Future* report (1976) urged closer links between local education, child guidance and psychiatric health services. Two years later, the wide-ranging Warnock Report advocated the controversial integration of most special-needs children into mainstream schools.

Brunswick Primary School parents and children protest (unsuccessfully) against the closure of their school due to falling rolls. Cambridge c. 1978.

It was also a significant decade for public-sector higher education, with major changes in structure, provision and salaries. The Robbins Report (1963) had led to unparalleled university expansion; more students passed GCE A-Levels, aspiring to degrees. New 'plate-glass' universities opened their doors in East Anglia, Sussex, Lancaster and Warwick. The 1972 White Paper predicted numbers would increase to approximately 750,000 students by 1981. The newly designated polytechnics, offering advanced vocational courses, were expected to absorb this growth; colleges of higher education similarly offered degree courses. The 1974 Houghton Report publicly acknowledged that lecturers' and schoolteachers' professionalism was inadequately rewarded compared to similar occupations. Its key recommendation of a salary increase of around 30 per cent was enthusiastically welcomed. However, within a few years, rapid inflation had quickly eroded this award.

A new journal, *The Times Higher Education Supplement*, reported a marked bias among university applicants towards the humanities: in 1971 around 10,000 applied for 2,200 arts and social sciences courses, yet only 2,700 for over 3,500 science places. 'Academic drift' meant the new polytechnics often replicated traditional humanities and social sciences degree courses, rather than advancing technological higher education. Additionally, the detrimental effect of high inflation on many families' incomes led to a decline in the number of eighteen-year-olds entering higher education: only 12.4 per cent by 1978 compared to 14.2 per cent six years earlier.

Dramatic change was also apparent in colleges of education. Financial stringency, and the falling birth rate, led to severe government cuts in initial teacher-training numbers. By the ıid-1970s, many colleges had amalgamated with polytechnics or ormed new institutions, offering different degree courses in addition o teacher training. Others were closed. In 1975, the popular Sidney Webb College of Education, providing valuable teacher training for nature students, became the Polytechnic of Central London's School of Education. Yet, after only two years, the government wound down his unique institution and its doors finally closed in 1980.

New degree routes gradually became available, especially for nature and part-time students. In 1971, the Open University (OU) enrolled its first intake; by 1979, sixty thousand students were ollowing new-style courses. A distance-learning institution with an pen-entry policy, the OU was noted for its innovatory teaching, earning materials and summer schools. In an age before video ecorders, its radio and TV programmes were, however, frequently proadcast at unsocial hours. Mature students, often in full-time mployment, also journeyed after work to Birkbeck College, University of London, to study for undergraduate courses or register or research degrees; others enrolled as external students. In 1976, the University College of Buckingham became the first British private nstitution to offer its own two-year degrees.

Higher education featured in 1970s British literature. Left-wing groups, dominant on many university campuses were satirised in Malcolm Bradbury's *The History Man* (1975), where the central character was a philandering Marxist lecturer. Greater knowledge of life in further education colleges, with their wide-ranging provision of vocational courses for sixteen- to nineteen-year-olds (e.g. hair dressing, cookery, nursery training, vehicle maintenance, information technology) was to be found in Tom Sharpe's comedic 1970s *Wilt* books. Set in the fictional

Helping stretch the comprehensive school budget. Jane Whiter, teacher at Swavesey Village College, buys second-hand books for the library, September 1979.

CAMBRIDGESHIRE COUNTY COUNCIL

The Chairman and Members of the Social Services Committee
cordially invite

Miss S. Foster.

to the opening of their elderly persons' home
at 15 Coronation Street (off Hills Road),
Cambridge on Friday 23 November 1979 at 3 pm,
by Mrs Jean Barker, former Mayor of Cambridge

RSVP   Social Services Department   TEA
       Hobson Street, Cambridge

An invitation to the opening of a new home for the elderly, Coronation Street, Cambridge, 23 November 1979.

Fenland College, they were loosely based on Cambridgeshire College of Arts and Technology, where the author had previously taught history to apprentices and day-release students.

Whatever the popular perceptions of student life, the 1970s began to break down Victorian gender divisions in higher education, even reaching the hallowed halls of Oxbridge. Between 1972 and 1974, a number of elite all-male colleges reluctantly began to admit women undergraduates; and in 1975 Cambridge University appointed its first woman vice-chancellor. However, promotion prospects for women in academic life still often remained limited.

By the 1970s, although those in work were achieving a better standard of living, the thirty-year-old welfare state was coming under increasing pressure. People were living longer; men had a life expectancy of sixty-seven years, while women could expect to live into their mid-seventies.

The governments of the 1970s introduced benefit changes. Some were beneficial. Home care allowances and pensions for the over-eighties rose; the age for widows' pension entitlement was lowered and a £10 pensioners' Christmas bonus was introduced. However, by targeting specific groups, the welfare system was becoming 'no longer comprehensive nor universal'.

The 1975 Social Security Pensions Act aimed to preserve women's pension rights if they were off work for domestic reasons. From 1978, a new state earnings-related pension scheme (SERPS) helped millions of low-paid workers without occupational or personal pensions. Benefits for the disabled and long-term sick were linked to earnings or prices, whichever was higher.

From 1971 there was a supplementary benefit, Family Income Settlement, for the lowest earners, but being means tested, it was often unpopular. Between 1972 and 1977, the number of families with incomes below the supplementary benefit level increased dramatically, forcing more children into poverty. A long campaign by The Child Poverty Action Group, with support from trade unions, churches and women's groups, led to child benefit replacing family and child tax allowances in 1979. Child benefit was paid in cash directly to the mother, providing some financial independence, but the change arguably left many fathers worse off as they lost a previously helpful child tax allowance.

Children's care homes also fell under the social services umbrella. In 1979, International Year of the Child, Cambridge Social Services appealed for foster parents for needy children 'at home in Britain'. Years later, scandals emerged nationwide about 1970s children's homes, suggesting many were at best too strict, at worst abusive. Actor Neil Morrissey recalled his Stoke-on-Trent care home, with 'strict shouty housemothers', where he was 'rarely cuddled'. A 2009 Radio 4 *Today* programme alleged that the regular use of tranquilisers for 'disturbed' girls in seventies' children's homes may have resulted in them giving birth to children with birth defects later in life.

The decade proved controversial for physically and mentally disabled patients in long-stay hospitals, whose care passed from the NHS to social services. Laudable aims to 'deinstitutionalise', by treating individuals in their own homes, sometimes resulted in vulnerable people being left with insufficient support; 'care in the community' appeared at times to be sadly inadequate.

The 'excessive' cost of state welfare was increasingly held responsible for the nation's ills. By the late 1970s, nearly a tenth of the population, mainly the unemployed, disabled and single parents, relied on social service benefits. Apocryphal systemic abuses filled the media – 'televisions on legs' claimed as furniture, or benefits spent by 'dole cheats' on 'best cigars'. While the 1978 NHS London conference was celebratory, a small social services display in Newcastle-upon-Tyne, depicting thirty years of social security, was attended by 'not many public and even fewer journalists'.

An old lady in her kitchen, waiting to be evicted from a tenement building, probably in London, September 1973.

NEW WAVE NEWS

40

WITH THE

SEX PISTOLS

ROTTE
POSTE
INSID

STRANGLERS   CLASH   DAMNE

RELAXATION AND
ENTERTAINMENT

RELAXATION AND ENTERTAINMENT provide an alternative and changing picture of British life in the 1970s. Increased leisure time could often provide respite during troubled times. For many, especially women, leisure, recreation and sport often meant simply 'time for one's self', rather than formal participation. Television figures rose as home viewing replaced visits to the cinema. Art, cultural events and pop concerts all attracted growing audiences. People were consumers of, and participants in, an increasing range of sporting events and activities.

Television became the nation's entertainment of choice. The lifting of restrictions on broadcasting led to rising viewing figures. In 1972, fifteen million people still watched in 'black and white' yet, by the mid-1970s, the price of colour television sets had dropped dramatically. Colour became available for all the three channels: BBC 1, BBC 2 and ITV.

It was a golden age for comedy on British television. Many popular programmes from this time have become familiar classics. Any poll of memorable productions would include *Porridge* and *Dad's Army*. In 2000, *Fawlty Towers* was voted the 'best programme in television history'. Top of the bill were Morecambe and Wise: twenty-nine million fans watched their 1977 Christmas show.

In 1971, *The Two Ronnies* began a popular run of over thirty years. *Last of The Summer Wine* (1973) and children's *John Craven's Newsround* (1972) were equally long-lasting. Memorable children's television also included *The Magic Roundabout* and *PlaySchool*. In 2008, *Bagpuss* (1974) was accorded 'best TV animal of all time'.

The more literary praised the impressive *I, Claudius* (1976) and Dennis Potter's *Pennies from Heaven* (1978), although the latter was heavily criticised by moral campaigner Mary Whitehouse. Memorable 'one-offs' included *Edna the Inebriate Woman* (1971). Later, Melvyn Bragg's acclaimed *South Bank Show* (1978) became the longest-running arts programme.

Opposite:
The Sex Pistols punk rock group on the front cover of *New Wave News*, late 1970s. Inside was a poster of Johnny Rotten, the Sex Pistols' lead singer from 1975 to 1978.

Board game inspired by the 1970s television sitcom *On The Buses*. Some external shots were filmed at the old Wood Green bus garage, north London. Film spin-offs included *Holiday On The Buses*, set in a Pontin's holiday camp.

The cast of *Death on the Nile* (1978) included Simon McCorkindale (fifth from left), David Niven, George Kennedy, Peter Ustinov, Lois Chiles, Bette Davis, Maggie Smith, and Angela Lansbury.

Despite competition from television, radio retained a devoted, albeit far smaller, following. Terry Wogan achieved unparalleled popularity on Radio 2. While Radio 1 dominated the ratings with its chart hits, Radio 3 provided classical music for a minority. For current affairs, *Today* on Radio 4 set a daily political agenda for listeners, with the programme, for a while, broadcast jointly from Manchester and

London. Proceedings in Parliament were broadcast from 1975, Scottish Gaelic Radio came from Stornaway (1979) and London Broadcasting Company (LBC), became Britain's first legal commercial independent radio station in 1973.

In difficult economic times, British cinema audiences dwindled, and many cinemas closed. Crucial US funding was withdrawn and two-thirds of Shepperton Studios was sold off. Weekends changed as children deserted 'Saturday morning pictures' for television; ratings for Noel Edmonds' *Multi-Coloured Swap Shop* on BBC I soared.

Nonetheless, there were some highly successful British films, including Agatha Christie adaptations with high-profile casts: *Murder on the Orient Express* (1974), also *Death on the Nile* (1978), which saw the rise to fame of the young Simon McCorkindale. The highly controversial *Straw Dogs* (1971) starred British actress Susan George (later McCorkindale's wife). Other memorable British films included *The Go-Between* (1970) and classic occult thriller *Don't Look Now* (1973). Michael Caine's *Get Carter* (1971) was famously set in Newcastle-upon-Tyne. The cutting-edge British Film Institute was prominent in the 1970s, the decade when British Asian and black films first appeared.

The Australian film industry made a stylish impact, notably with *Picnic At Hanging Rock* (1975). However, it was the American movie that swept Britain with *The Godfather* (1972), *Jaws* (1975) and *Apocalypse Now* (1979), while the original *Star Wars* (1977) established a cult following. British technicians found a small niche in American studios, providing special effects for *Superman* and *Alien*. In 1977, the world mourned British-born international silent-screen star, Charlie Chaplin.

The 1970s engendered enormous interest in the arts. Numbers visiting galleries and museums soared; two million queued for hours to see the 1972 Tutankhamun Exhibition. In 1977 the Tate Art Gallery's appeal saved two George Stubbs paintings for the nation; David Hockney's *Mr and Mrs Clark and Percy* became an enduring image. The controversy over the Tate's 1972 purchase of Carl Andre's 'pile of bricks' (*Equivalent VIII*) raged for years.

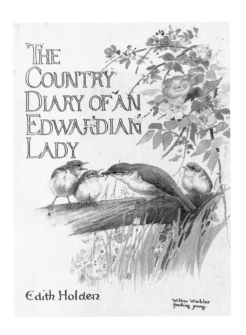

THE COUNTRY DIARY OF AN EDWARDIAN LADY

Edith Holden

Willow Warbler feeding young.

A triumph for nostalgia, *The Country Diary of an Edwardian Lady*, written by Edith Holden in 1906 as *Nature Notes*, was posthumously published in 1977, becoming a huge success.

In 1976, the magnificent new National Theatre opened on London's South Bank. With three separate auditoria, it staged, among other works, several Peter Hall productions including *The Tempest* Harold Pinter's *No Man's Land* and *Bedroom Farce* by Alan Ayckbourn then in his heyday. Agatha Christie's *The Mousetrap* celebrated its silver anniversary at St Martin's Theatre in 1977; Tom Stoppard became the 'decade's theatrical dazzler'. 'Sex musical' *Oh Calcutta!* appeared in 1970; *Jesus Christ Superstar* (1978) later became the longest-running British musical. Women's theatre groups flourished on the fringe Black theatre companies also developed, including Talawa. In 2010, Talawa began recording interviews with black actors from the seventies on their recollections of the theatre at that time.

The Paddington Bear toy first appeared in 1972. Gabrielle Designs, run by Shirley and Eddie Clarkson, made a prototype bear for their children Joanna and Jeremy Clarkson (later famous motoring journalist).

In the literary world, publishing suffered from the collapsing economy, with talk of the end of the English novel. Sales of hardbacks dwindled as cheaper paperbacks became more commercial. The House of Lords debated the plight of low-earning authors although the amendment of lending rights, with small returns on library loans, improved their situation somewhat. In 1973, the British Library was created.

The top-selling book of 1970 was John Fowles' *The French Lieutenant's Woman*; in 1978, Iris Murdoch's *The Sea, the Sea* won the Booker Prize. Some writers began to tackle racism. *Spare Rib*, the feminist magazine, appeared in 1972, although WH Smith determinedly refused to stock it. The radical women's publisher, Virago, was launched in 1974; four years later Islington's Sisterwrite became the 'ultimate feminist bookshop'. In poetry, Ted Hughes' impressive 1970 collection, *Crow*, and the popular 1972 appointment of Sir John Betjeman as Poet Laureate were celebrated, but the death of W. H. Auden in 1973 marked the end of an era.

In many schools, creativity was at the centre of the curriculum. A 1979 *Observer* schools collage competition, including sixteen-year-old Debra Livingstone's highly commended *Delegation,* toured Britain, starting at Euston Station, London's 'most modern terminal'. Other children made their own cine films; at Christchurch Primary School, Barnet, real locations were used, with children providing scripts, sets and music. Despite the incursion of television into British homes, reading remained popular for many children.

Puffin Book Club membership reached fifty thousand. In 1972, Enid Blyton still remained the most popular author for young children. The phenomenally successful *Watership Down* (Richard Adams, 1972), and *Masquerade* (Kit Williams, 1979), appealed to adults as well as children. Children's toys included Chopper bikes, space hoppers, skateboards and Smurfs, also seen on wallpaper; in 1972, the first Paddington Bear toy appeared. Corgi, Dinky and Matchbox toy cars suffered from fierce American competition but Scalextric built on the success of British Formula One racing champion, James Hunt, by producing a toy model of his car.

The 'pop'-dominated musical decade began with the Beatles' spectacular break-up and the first Glastonbury Festival. Music fairs and festivals were attended by thousands of fans, listening to a range of popular music: disco, funk, rock and punk. Sales of vinyl records soared. Young 'teeny boppers' caught 'Osmania' as American Jimmy Osmond's 'Longhaired Lover from Liverpool' topped the charts (1973). Glam Rock stars, Elton John, Gary Glitter and David Bowie, dazzled with sequins, nail varnish, and colourful hair. Anti-establishment punk rock developed mid-decade. The Sex Pistols, with singer Johnny Rotten and bassist Sid Vicious, shocked the establishment by defying social norms, yet in 1977 they gave a concert for the children of striking Huddersfield firemen.

In the north-east, working-class girls' marching jazz bands were a common sight; one appeared in the film *Get Carter*. In 1977, devastated fans in Britain and across the world mourned the death of legendary idol Elvis Presley. A world away from pop, English composer Benjamin Britten died (1976) and a 1912 song, *The Floral Dance*, became a huge hit in 1978 when broadcaster Terry Wogan recorded his own unique version.

During the 1970s, the beginnings of late-twentieth-century commercialism gradually infiltrated spectator sport, particularly football, golf and motor racing. Millions also watched sport on television, instead of listening to it on the radio. At the same time, leisure shopping and 'days out with the car' took thousands away from gate-money sports. Long-standing social and class distinctions, such as 'amateur' and 'professional', embodied in cricket, tennis and athletics,

Left: Cambridge's Strawberry Fair, Midsummer Common, 1978. Begun in 1974, and still running in 2011, it provided music, entertainment and arts-and-crafts stalls.

Standing-only ticket for the 1978 final of the World Individual Speedway Championship, Empire Stadium, Wembley. World Speedway finals were held at Wembley throughout the 1970s.

began to disappear.

While football retained pre-eminence as Britain's national sport, especially with England's 1966 World Cup Wembley victory, the numbers watching their much-loved football team on a Saturday afternoon dwindled over the decade, never matching post-war heights. However there were still dedicated fans who attended regularly, as depicted in Nick Hornby's classic *Fever Pitch* (1992), which captured the highs and lows of his life as a passionate Arsenal fan during the 1970s.

In 1970, England's national football team lost in the Mexico World Cup quarter-finals and failed to even qualify in 1974 and 1978. Sir Alf Ramsey, knighted when his team became world champions, was sacked in 1974, as were his successors when England failed to recapture world supremacy. The death of sixty-six Rangers fans at Glasgow's Ibrox Park, January 1971, was an unforgettable tragedy but led to the emergence of all-seater stadia. Throughout the decade, hooliganism, often exaggerated by tabloid sensationalism, dogged the 'beautiful game'.

The numbers watching sport on television steadily grew. The annual tennis tournament at Wimbledon was especially popular. Millions saw the first black player to win a Wimbledon title, Arthur Ashe, achieve the singles in 1975. In 1978, ITV challenged the supremacy of BBC sport, gaining the right to broadcast recorded highlights of football league matches on Saturday nights. The growing regard for televised sports was reflected in the number of broadcasters who became household names: Jimmy Hill, Barry Davies, Brian Moore, John Motson (football), Harry Carpenter (boxing), Dan Maskell (tennis), Alan Weeks (ice-skating) and David Coleman (athletics).

At the same time, grass-roots sports in local parks, sports centres and clubs expanded. Football, golf, tennis, cricket, bowls and darts were amongst the more popular activities. New 'lifestyle' sports, such as jogging, aerobics and yoga became fashionable. Notably, more women participated in sport, often inspired by the achievements of elite 1960s and 1970s performers like Lilian Board (athletics), Ann Jones and Virginia Wade (tennis). 'Long live Queen Ginny' ran an ecstatic *Daily Mirror* headline when Virginia Wade won the Wimbledon women's singles championship in Jubilee year, 1977. Nevertheless, considerable gender inequalities remained, either with lower financial rewards for star female performers or fewer opportunities for women to partake. On 19 December 1978, the *Daily Mail* reported: 'FA bans two thirteen-year-old girls' from playing in a mixed football team.

The triumphant Arsenal football team tour Highbury, north London, in a double-decker bus after beating Manchester United (3-2) in the FA Cup Final on 12 May 1979.

There were British successes in ice-skating, sailing, and motor racing. Crowds flocked to Aintree to watch the legendary horse, Red Rum, win the Grand National three times. Following Tony Jacklin's 1970 US Open Championship success, golf in Britain was at its most popular since the 1920s, resulting in long waiting-lists for club memberships. However, rapid inflation often prevented the construction of expensive new courses. Instead, young professional men and women turned to squash as numerous new courts opened throughout the decade.

In the early 1970s, mesmerising Alex 'Hurricane' Higgins, 'working-class Belfast genius', took snooker by storm. From 1977, the World Snooker Championship was televised from the Sheffield Crucible, capturing a new audience. While cycling popularity declined, the arrival of the mountain bike launched a nationwide phenomenon by the end of the decade. Speedway motor-bike racing was on the wane, but a passionate minority still followed the sport.

By the end of the decade, public sports facilities had vastly improved, with the opening of new 'multi-purpose sportsdromes', floodlit dry ski-runs and leisure complexes. In 1973, Huddersfield's brand-new £900,000 Sports Centre was opened by international equestrian, Princess Anne, who two years earlier had been named BBC Sports Personality of the Year.

PLACES TO VISIT

Bus Preservation Trust Ltd, Redhill Road, Cobham, Surrey KT11 1EF
Tel: 01932 868665 www.lbpt.org

Colman's Mustard Shop and Museum, 15 Royal Arcade, Norwich NR2 1NQ
Tel: 01603 627889 www.mustardshopnorwich.co.uk

East Anglia Transport Museum, Chapel Road, Carlton Colville, Lowestoft,
Suffolk NR33 8BL Tel: 01502 518459 / 01502 584658
www.eatm.org.uk

Fashion and Textile Museum, 83, Bermondsey Street, London SE1 3XF
Tel: 0207 74078664 www.ftmlondon.org

Lakeland Motor Museum, Old Blue Mill, Backbarrow Ulverston, Cumbria
LA12 8TA Tel: 01539 530400
www.lakelandandmotormuseum.co.uk

London Transport Museum, 39 Wellington Street, London WC2E 7BB
Tel: 0207 3796344 www.ltmuseum.co.uk

Lord's Cricket Museum, St John's Wood Road, Grace Gate, London
NW8 8QN Tel: 0207 6168595
www.touruk.co.uk/london_museums/lordscricket_museum

Museum of British Road Transport, Hales Street, Coventry CV1 1PN
Tel: 0247 6832425 www.mbrt.co.uk

Museum of Power & Industry, Hatfield Road, Langford, Maldon, Essex
CM9 6QA
Tel: 01621 843183 www.museumofpower.org.uk

Museum of Science and Industry, Liverpool Road, Castlefield, Manchester
M3 4FP Tel: 0161 832 2244
www.mosi.org.uk/visiting-us/where-we-are.aspx

National Football Museum, Sir Tom Finney Way, Preston, PR1 6PA
Tel: 01772 908421 www.nationalfootballmuseum.com

National Horse Racing Museum, 99 High Street, Newmarket, Suffolk
CB8 8JH Tel: 01638 667333
www.nhrm.co.uk

National Maritime Museum Cornwall, Discovery Quay, Falmouth TR11
Tel: 01326 313388 www.nmmc.co.uk

National Motor Cycle Museum, Coventry Road, Bickenhill, Solihull,
West Midlands B92 0EJ
Tel: 01675 443311 www.nationalmotorcyclemuseum.co.uk

National Motor Museum, John Montagu Building, Beaulieu, Brockenhurst,
Hampshire, SO42 7ZN
Tel: 01590 612345 www.beaulieu.co.uk

National Railway Museum, Leeman Road, York YO26 4XJ
Tel: 08448 15 3139 www.nrm.org.uk

eople's History Museum, Left Bank, Spinningfields, Manchester M3 3ER
   Tel: 0161 838 9190 www.phm.org.uk
   Trades union, Labour and Co-operative history.

obert Opie Museum, Colville Mews, Lonsdale Road, Notting Hill, London
   W11 2AR Tel: 0207 9080880
   Museum of brands, packaging and advertising.

S Great Britain, Great Western Dockyard, Bristol BS1 6TY
   Tel: 0117 926 0680 www.ssgreatbritain.org/visit

ictoria & Albert Museum, South Kensington, Cromwell Road, London
   SW7 2RL Tel: 0207 7942 2000 www.vam.ac.uk
   Art and design museum.

Wimbledon Lawn Tennis Museum, All England Lawn Tennis & Croquet Club,
   Church Road, Wimbledon SW19 5AE Tel: 0208 946 6131
   www.wimbledon.org

INDEX

*Page numbers in italic
refer to illustrations*